Practical Communication

2nd Edition

Practical Communication

25 Tips, Tools, and Techniques for Getting Along and Getting Things Done

2nd Edition

Amy Castro

ICTS PRESS
FRIENDSWOOD, TEXAS

Copyright © 2016 by Amy Castro

ICTS PRESS
Friendswood, TX 77546
www.ICTSPress.com

ISBN: 978-1536832914

Printed in the United States of America

Contents

Acknowledgments

ALTHOUGH there are too many to name here, I thank all the people over the years who encouraged me to write a book that would build on what they've learned in my programs. Thanks also to all the friends who supported me throughout the process.

Special appreciation goes to my editor, Bryan Grossman, for bearing with me as I sent him chapters in various stages of completion, and for making me sound like a better writer than I am. Additionally, I thank my dear friends Bev Brooks, and Barry, Penny, and Stacy Grossman for lending their editing and communication expertise as well as confirmation that such a book was needed and of use.

Finally, I thank my husband, LeRoy, and my daughter, Kelsey, for their patience as I worked on this book instead of doing any number of things I promised to get done—including tonight's late dinner as I write this acknowledgment.

Introduction

IMAGINE passing a home under construction and watching the carpenter attempt to build the house with only a hammer and screwdriver. He might be able to get some of the tasks done but certainly not all of them, and he would be unable to achieve his goal. The solution: adding to his toolbox in order to build a set of tools that allows him to reach his goal successfully.

When it comes to communication, our parents issued us our toolbox; they're the ones who first taught us to communicate. Our tools are likely limited. They may have allowed us to survive to this point, but are we able to accomplish everything we want to with limited tools? Probably not. If we were lucky, we collected a few new tools along the way as we grew and interacted with others, but still, we're likely a bit ill-equipped.

Communication is something most of us take for granted. We've been communicating since we were born. When we were hungry, wet, or tired, we cried, and our parents responded. As we grew, our parents and then our teachers taught us to speak, read, and write so we could communicate more clearly. Unfortunately, true interpersonal communication skills—those skills used to interact one-on-one—aren't usually taught at home or at school. Take for example, listening skills. Someone may have told us, "Shut up, and listen." However, were we ever told how to listen effectively beyond keeping our mouths shut? Probably not. The same goes for choosing our words; someone probably told us certain words were good or bad, appropriate or inappropriate, but beyond that, did we have lessons on choosing words that best impact the listener, or how to most clearly state our message? Again, probably not.

If our parents happened to be fairly good communicators, then our skills might be fairly good. If our parents were less-than-stellar communicators, then we might be going through life damaging our personal and working relationships with unclear communication. Therefore, we move forward from childhood into the adult world with a limited set of interpersonal communication tools.

9

The purpose of this book is not to serve as a communication textbook, teaching you human communication theory and drilling communication research into your brain. The purpose, rather, is to help you add to your communication toolbox, so you will be able to communicate successfully at work. However, all the tools presented can also be used when communicating with family, friends, and others you encounter throughout your day. Each chapter contains one straightforward communication tool. It's possible you already possess some of the tools and just need a reminder to pull them out of your toolbox and use them more often. Other tools might be new to you and a welcome addition to your skill set. Additionally, each chapter ends with recommendations that will allow you to ACT on what you've learned: Analyze current behaviors, Communicate using the new skill from the chapter, and refer to the Tips for successfully implementing the new skill. Add one skill at a time, work on it until it becomes a habit, and by the time you finish reading this book, you'll have a much more complete set of communication tools for dealing with the people and situations you encounter every day.

Chapter 1

Communication Without Words

THE focus of this book is to provide words and phrases that help create a friendly productive work environment where we can get along and get things done. In fact, we can use these tools in many situations, from interactions with family and friends, to communicating in situations where we are the customer. So why a chapter on communication without words? Shouldn't it all be about talking? Our society seems to think so. The squeaky wheel gets the grease, after all. We're a society of talkers. It starts almost at birth—adults loom in our faces urging us to speak our first words. It's no wonder we value talk so much and spend so much time doing it. Unfortunately, no matter how well you choose your words, if you don't recognize the importance of nonverbal communication and silence in your messages, your communication won't be effective. Whether in a face-to-face situation or over the telephone, what is said without words can be just as critical, if not more so, than the words themselves.

Nonverbal Communication

First, let's talk about nonverbal communication. Nonverbal communication consists of body language, such as facial expressions, eye contact, hand gestures, posture, and touch, as well as our vocal qualities, such as volume, pitch, and rate of speech. When we deliver a message with the "wrong" nonverbals, the message will be lost and the nonverbals become the focus.

To begin the process of improving communication, we must recognize that no matter how great the words, how perfect our script, if our nonverbals don't support the message, the message becomes not what we say, but rather how we say it. It's very important to pay attention to *how* we say things and *what* we're doing while saying them, so we can identify what messages we're really sending.

For example, if we ran into someone we really liked and hadn't seen in a while, we'd probably say, "It's great to see you!" We would smile, make direct eye contact, and possibly give the person a hug. Our voices would likely be loud, sincere, enthusiastic, and without hesitation. Nonverbal messages can either reinforce the verbal message, or contradict it. In this case, all of our nonverbals tell the long-lost friend the same thing: "I'm really happy to see you."

Now imagine a scenario where we unexpectedly run into someone we don't like. We might use the same words as in the previous scenario because we want to be polite. However, those words won't come across the same way they did to our long-lost friend. Because we really aren't happy to see this person, our nonverbals will likely reflect that. Although we may lie with our words, it's much harder to lie with our nonverbals because they are a result of what we're really thinking and feeling. Therefore, unless we're good actors, the truth will come out and our real feelings become obvious. "Oh, uh, hi, (pause) it's so great to see you," said with a flat, monotone voice, unhappy facial expression, no smile, and wavering eye contact tells the person, "Darn, I wish I hadn't run into you. What can I do to get out of here?"

Nonverbal communication plays a significant role in either reinforcing or contradicting our words. An oft-quoted statistic states that 93 percent of our communication is nonverbal—this is an oversimplification of the research upon which it is based. However, it's fair to say that our nonverbal messages are critical to the believability of our words. Our cultural clichés reflect this reality: "Actions speak louder than words," and "It's not what you say, but how you say it."

Here are some nonverbal communication tips that will help you successfully implement the verbal communication tools in this book:

1. Match the nonverbal to the message.
2. Take note of thoughts and feelings before speaking.
3. Realize that nonverbal communication is situational.
4. Make a point of using nonverbals that strengthen your message.
5. Realize that nonverbal communication varies across cultures.
6. Pay attention to what others' nonverbals are telling you, but be cautious about over-interpreting their meaning.

1. Match the nonverbal to the message.

Nonverbals that send messages that are consistent with the words used serve to reinforce those words. If we're sending a serious message, we need to look and sound serious.

We can't tell someone, "If you don't come in on time tomorrow, I'll need to write you up," while looking at our shoes, stumbling over our words, whispering, and avoiding eye contact. We need to speak firmly and without hesitation, look the person directly in the eye, and sound as if we mean what we're saying.

2. Take note of thoughts and feelings before speaking.

If we want to sound confident but feel terrified, at best we'll come across as insecure. The mindset and emotion must match the words. The same goes for when we're angry or upset about something, but want to discuss the problem calmly without sounding angry or upset. We're not going to pull it off, because the anger will likely prevail through our nonverbal communication. It may be best to wait until our thoughts and feelings are more congruent with what we're trying to say.

3. Realize that nonverbal communication is situational.

A strong tone meant to tell someone, "I mean it!" might be read as assertive by one person, and misinterpreted by another as anger or frustration. Additionally, nonverbals can take on different connotations depending on the situation. For example, the strong tone we might use when telling children at home, "I mean it," may be completely inappropriate at work or in a social situation. Therefore, we may need to adjust our nonverbals for different situations and people.

4. Make a point of using nonverbals that strengthen your message.

When planning to communicate with someone, think about nonverbals that will reinforce your messages as well as those to avoid that might weaken the message. In general, use nonverbals that send the same message as your words. If you're truly sorry, your face should appear apologetic. You shouldn't be smiling or smirking. If you're truly happy for someone who just got promoted, your voice should sound excited and happy, your eyes should be wide and alert, and you should smile. You shouldn't speak in monotone or wear a pained expression on your face.

5. Realize that nonverbal communication varies across cultures.

Americans view eye contact as a tremendous indicator of sincerity, honesty, and confidence. As such, most require eye contact in order to take interactions seriously. Keep in mind though, the use of eye contact, and in fact many nonverbal messages, mean different things in different cultures. Although we can't know the nonverbal "rules" of every culture, when interacting with others, we should be aware that they might not operate under the same nonverbal rules as we do. Additionally, when we're in social or work situations where we know we'll be interacting with people from different cultures, it's a good idea to become familiar with some of their customs, not only so that we can better read them, but to allow us to adjust our nonverbals accordingly.

6. *Pay attention to what others' nonverbals are telling you, but be cautious about over-interpreting their meaning.*

Just as your nonverbals communicate to others, their nonverbals are communicating to you. When talking with people, even on the telephone, listen carefully to what their nonverbals are telling you. Are they sending contradicting messages from their words? Do the nonverbals reveal something about how the person is feeling or what he or she may really think?

However, we shouldn't make the mistake of believing that by reading others' nonverbals we can read their hearts and minds. Nonverbal behaviors can often have more than one interpretation. We will explore this further in Chapter 5.

Silence is Golden

Not many people realize that silence is a very powerful communication tool—sometimes even more powerful than nonverbal communication or words.

Doubt it? Try this. Look a person in the eye, ask him or her a question, and then wait for a response. Remain silent and simply maintain eye contact and provide your undivided attention.

What happens? He or she will talk, elaborate, confess (especially kids), reveal, and otherwise share things you would never have heard if you were talking.

Silence is affirming to the speaker and a tremendous learning tool for the listener. We're not talking about the blank stare, "I'm-not-really-listening" type of silence—rather "engaged silence," where we give a person our undivided attention and keep our mouths shut, except to prompt them to say more.

Engaged silence shows people we are interested in what they have to say. Since so many people focus on talking, it's uncommon to have the uninterrupted attention of another person. When we do, we feel valued and appreciate that rare listener. People who use silence effectively create an opportunity to learn something they never would have if they had done most of the talking.

What does this customer really want?

What's really bothering my coworker?

Why is my boss so frustrated about this project?

We'll never know if we're too busy talking about what we can and can't do, what's bothering us, and sharing our own frustrations.

For those of us who are big talkers, silence will be difficult to maintain at first. We'll want to interrupt, add our opinions, and otherwise take over the conversation. If we resist the urge to jump in, we will likely be very surprised by what we learn and how much those around us appreciate our full attention.

ACT on this chapter

Analyze: Think about times in the past when communication has gone wrong. How many times do you think the miscommunication occurred because of missed or contradicting nonverbal cues? How many times was there miscommunication because everyone was talking, but no one was listening or giving another person the chance to have his or her "say"?

Communicate: In the coming weeks, before worrying about what to say, take some time to think about how you'll say it. What nonverbal messages are you going to send? Also, pay close attention to the messages others are communicating without speaking. You'll find there's a lot more communication going on behind those words. Take opportunities to give up the stage to those around you. Ask questions when appropriate, then give your undivided, silent attention as people respond. It may be a challenge at first, but you'll be amazed by what you'll learn. If you're a big talker, the people around you will also be amazed that you've really become interested in them instead of yourself.

Tips: Learn to "read" what others mean, and when in doubt, *ask*. For others to take your nonverbals to heart, be sure your nonverbals reinforce the message you're trying to communicate with your words. To avoid interrupting others or "stage hogging" take notes on what they're saying. If you're having trouble paying attention while remaining silent, instead of thinking about what you'll say next, paraphrase in your mind what you're hearing. Think about questions you'll want to ask when it's your turn to speak.

Chapter 2

What's the Magic Word?

PLEASE. What better place to start than with one of the most basic of courtesies? Please—a simple word that shouldn't require a reminder. Our mothers demanded it when we were children. "What's the magic word?" "What do we say when we want someone to pass the broccoli?" "No thanks," perhaps.

As we get older, move out on our own, and no longer rely on our mothers to keep us in line, many of us stop using the word "please" and rather imply it. We use our vocal qualities—a pleasant tone, a slight raise in pitch at the end of a request—to indicate "please."

Recall how it sounds when we've heard phrases such as the following:

"Could you pass the ketchup?"

"Would you call me back as soon as you can?"

"Can you write me a recommendation for the promotion?"

Although often accepted as a substitute for "please," a pleasant tone alone may not be enough. Keep in mind, inflection and tone only work when the listener hears and interprets them as the speaker intended. What happens when someone can't hear our tone or misinterprets it?

For example, an employee leaves a telephone message for a client, "I need to get your signature on the proposal before I can submit it to my boss. Call me back when you get a chance." If the speaker's tone is not pleasant enough, the raised pitch at the end doesn't imply a request, or the telephone connection is bad and the caller can't hear the person's vocal qualities, the client may interpret this message as rude or even demanding.

Additionally, because we conduct so much of our business communication through e-mail, the word "please" is even more important. When we send emails, others can't hear our voices or see our facial expressions, so the message they receive is incomplete. What do receivers do when they only receive an incomplete message? Fill in the blanks, of course.

This is why we often perceive an angry tone, even if the writer doesn't say he or she is angry, or we read sarcasm into a question or comment. By leaving the word "please" out of an e-mail, what we intended to be a request turns into a demand. "Send me your input by Thursday," comes across as SEND ME YOUR INPUT BY THURSDAY ... OR ELSE!"

To avoid being perceived as angry or rude, simply remember what Mom always said: Use the magic word in face-to-face, phone, and e-mail communication.

ACT on this chapter

Analyze: Look back on the past few weeks and think about times when someone asked you to help, but didn't say please. Did you feel as if you were being bossed around? Did it make you reluctant to help? Also, consider the times you took for granted that the "please" you meant to say was implied by your tone. Are you sure the "please" was heard?

Communicate: Take every opportunity you can to say "please" in person and in writing. If necessary, set a goal for saying "please" at least five times each day. By the end of the week, you will be well on your way to turning politeness into a renewed habit. Your friends, coworkers, employees, and customers will appreciate it.

Tips: The sincerity of your request will likely be judged not just by saying please but also by how you say it. Be sure your nonverbals convey the sincerity you feel when you say "please." Also, when sending requests via e-mail, be sure to double check your messages before you send them to ensure they sound like requests, not demands. When you read them, think about how you'd interpret the message if you were the receiver. Do you "feel" the sincerity coming through? If not, consider changing the words or the order of items so that you send the right message. Finally, on a side note: E-mail "emoticons" are not a replacement for please and generally should not be used in business correspondence, as they may come across as unprofessional at best, and at worst may be misunderstood. Is that winking smiley face indicating the e-mail sender is kidding or trying to flirt?

Chapter 3

Thank You

USUALLY, when someone provides a service, favor, or courtesy, many return the courtesy with a "thanks."

"Thanks for passing the ketchup."

"Thanks for calling me back."

"Thanks for copying me on that sales e-mail."

In these and other similar instances, a mere thanks—although more informal than the full thank you—is sufficient.

Unfortunately, there are instances when thanks is not only insufficient but can have the exact opposite intended effect. Instead of the recipient feeling appreciated, he or she may feel unappreciated, angry, and very unwilling to do anything to help us again. "Thanks for passing the ketchup" works whereas, "Thanks for the kidney," seems to fall short.

Imagine being the recipient of the outpouring of appreciation below when you worked for two weeks, through your lunch hour, to help a colleague who fell behind in his research.

"I got those statistics you sent. Thanks."

Would you be likely to put forth that kind of effort again? When someone gives more than the minimal effort, is inconvenienced by helping us out, or donates a body part, a more thorough and meaningful thank you is required.

A sincere and meaningful thank you contains three parts:

1. A specific description of the person's words and/or actions, including any "sacrifice" that may have been involved for the person in doing the task.
2. A description of the positive results or outcome of their actions.
3. Actually saying the words "thank you" either at the beginning or end of the comments.

"Mary, I want to thank you for getting these statistics to me. I know you had to work through your lunch hour all week to get them to me by the deadline. Your willingness to take the time to get me the information was a key factor in us getting the XYZ contract."

How would Mary feel, after sacrificing her lunch hour for a week, having her colleague look her in the eye and sincerely stating the above sentiments? She'd probably feel great. It's also likely that she'd be willing to make a sacrifice for this person again because her hard work was acknowledged and truly appreciated.

ACT on this chapter

Analyze: Think about all the people around you whose actions support you and help you to be successful. From the administrative assistant who sets up the conference room for your meeting to the child at home who empties the dishwasher without complaining, every person needs to know that what they do is appreciated. It doesn't matter if the task is in their job description or on their list of chores, a little appreciation goes a long way and will make them feel great, increasing the odds they will willingly help you the next time.

Communicate: From the extraordinary to the mundane, take every opportunity in the coming weeks to show sincere appreciation to those around you. Write a handwritten thank you note or send an e-mail to someone, including a copy to his or her boss. Call people into your office, look them in the eye, and provide sincere, detailed thank you's.

Tips: Be sure your expressions of appreciation include the right level of detail so the people receiving them know exactly what they did that you appreciate. Vague thank you's without detail can become meaningless, as they are often perceived as obligatory. However, there's no need to write and deliver a ten-minute thank you speech because someone passes you a paperclip. As with many communication techniques, sincerity and realism are the keys to an effective thank you.

Chapter 4

No!

FOR many of us, it's the first word we learn, thus the popularity of baby t-shirts that read, "My name is No No," on the front. We learn to use "no" first because it's a powerful word synonymous with taking a stand, contradicting authority, being an individual. "No, I won't take a bath!"

It was so easy to say as a child, so why do many of us stop using the word? Because there are consequences for saying "no." As children, when we told our parents we didn't want to take a bath, somehow we still ended up in the tub. If we said "no" to going to sleep, miraculously we ended up in our beds at night. Children who say "no" are usually overridden by someone bigger and with more authority. Consequences might also include a scolding or punishment for disobeying. The person who was bigger, stronger, more powerful, or more persistent got the last word and "won."

The lesson we learn is that "no" doesn't really work because there is always someone more powerful to override us. We also learn that when we do take a chance and say "no," we often get a negative reaction from the other person, such as hurt or anger. Therefore, we seek alternatives, such as avoidance, vagueness, or just giving in and saying yes. But do these options provide the best result for us or the other person? Not likely. Someone is going to end up unhappy. If we avoid the other person or are vague with our commitments, saying, "I'll check my schedule and get back with you"—and we never do—the other person is going to be unhappy. If we say yes all the time, we're going to be unhappy.

Saying "no" comes down to cost versus benefit analysis. "What's the cost of saying 'no'?" "What's the benefit to me if I say 'no'?" In addition, if we're nice people, we'll conduct a cost versus benefit analysis for saying "yes."

"What's the cost to me if I say 'yes'?" "What's the benefit to the other person if I say 'yes'?"

What we need to do is balance our needs with the needs of others, analyze the consequences of "yes" versus "no," and when the analysis is done, make the best decision. When we weigh our options and the scale is still evenly balanced, we'll need to decide what's more important—saying "yes" and meeting the other person's needs, or saying "no" and meeting our own.

The first step to recovering our ability to say "no" is to ask what we're afraid of and whether the fear is legitimate or exaggerated.

- ***Susan is going to hate me if I tell her I can't help with writing the proposal.*** Would she really hate someone who couldn't help this one time?

- ***I'll lose my job if I tell my boss I can't stay late today because I have a dentist appointment.*** Will the boss really fire someone if this is the first time he or she isn't able to stay late?

- ***Laura will be devastated if I tell her I can't go to her promotion party.*** Will she really be devastated? Will she be so upset that she won't be able to get out of bed that day? Or will she just be disappointed?

- ***Tara will be disappointed that I'm not going to be at the meeting.*** Okay, so she's disappointed. Sometimes people will be disappointed with our decisions. If we're doing the right thing, then we'll both have to live with it.

Some fears are legitimate but still worth facing by saying "no". For example, Tara may be disappointed that Donna is unable to attend the meeting. However, the potential for negative feelings needs to be weighed against what is right for the decision-maker. Sometimes the scales weigh in favor of declining a request. We need to say "no" while keeping in mind our best interests, our customers' best interests, or our family's best interests. The result might be that a friend, coworker, or boss is disappointed or unhappy.

Many people avoid saying "no" because they're afraid to cause others to feel unhappy or angry. This is a misconception. Individuals create their own happiness, sadness, and every other emotion. We don't make others unhappy. They make themselves unhappy. Our actions just trigger a thought process and that thought process creates the feeling of unhappiness. If the person on the receiving end of a "no" thinks, "Donna let me down," then that person is going to be disappointed. However, if the person being denied were to think, "It's too bad Donna isn't here, but I'm glad she's getting her tooth fixed; it must be very painful," then that person will likely be content with the situation.

Feelings don't come from outside sources. We create them in our own minds. Therefore, only the person receiving the message can control the emotional result. Because the people interpreting the message create feelings—both positive and negative—and because disappointment is human nature, people are going to be disappointed. It is essential to:

- *Do what we think is right* based on the situation.

- *Accept the decision* and the fact that disappointment could be the result.

- *Accept the result* and let the person making the request live with the disappointment. That person will likely get over it.

Sometimes, saying "no" isn't the right choice because the costs outweigh the benefits. For example, if we have evidence or a rational belief that our boss will fire us if we don't work late and we need the job, then it might be better to reschedule that dental appointment and work late.

However, in many instances, our fears are exaggerated or untrue. Susan and Tara might be angry or disappointed in the previously mentioned situations. If we're concerned about their feelings, we should weigh the costs of their potential angst against the reason we're denying their request, so we can make the "best" decision. Once we make the decision to say "no," the Susans, Lauras, and Taras of the world will have to live with the decision, and it's likely they'll realize that, like the child who refuses to go to bed, we don't always get what we want.

Assuming we can get over our fear of declining another's request, there are three basic ways to do it:

1. Say "no" and then be quiet.
2. Say "no" and offer an honest explanation.
3. Say "no" and offer an alternative.

1. Say "no" and then be quiet.

The first way to say "no" is to say it without explanations or alternatives. This is the best option when we don't plan to fulfill the request now or ever. People sometimes think it's politer to offer an excuse—true or not—to make the refusal easier to accept. The problem with offering an excuse or explanation is the likelihood of a counteroffer or follow-up question:

> **Martin**: "I really messed up. I spent so much time shopping for golf clubs online yesterday that I didn't finish my progress report for the week. Any chance you can come in this weekend and give me a hand? I have to have it done by Monday."
>
> **Lee:** "Hey man, I'm really sorry, but I coach my daughter's basketball team and we have two games on Saturday."
>
> **Martin:** "Okay. Well what about Sunday?"
>
> **Lee:** "Sorry, my grandma's birthday is Sunday so we're taking her out to lunch."
>
> **Martin:** "Well what time will you be done with that? Can you come later in the afternoon?"

Before Lee knows it, he'll run out of excuses. Then he'll find himself on Sunday afternoon helping Martin finish the progress report and resenting it, especially because Martin could have finished it if he hadn't wasted time shopping for golf clubs.

Therefore, in many instances, it's just better to say no and then be quiet.

"I'm sorry, I can't."

"No, thank you."

"I can't. I have another commitment."

If said with a pleasant tone, many people will accept refusal as long as it's straightforward, honest, and polite.

If Lee had simply replied, "I'm sorry, I can't," that likely would have been the end of it. If Martin follows up and asks why, Lee can simply say, "I have another commitment this weekend," and leave it at that. The phrase "I have another commitment" works well because it implies importance but doesn't provide enough detail to allow the other person to counter with an alternative. It also works in this situation because Martin's report is due on Monday. He doesn't have the option to propose another date to Lee.

2. Say "no" and offer an honest explanation.

The second way of saying "no" is to decline and offer an explanation. This method is simple when the explanation is true and palatable to the listener.

Martin: "I've fallen behind on my progress report. Any chance you can come in and give me a hand this weekend?"

Lee: "I'm sorry I can't. I'm leaving today for the annual conference in California and won't be back until next Sunday."

Declining a request when the listener won't like the reason is much more difficult. However, this type of explanation may be necessary if the request is likely to recur.

Frank: "Donna, would you like to go out on a date Friday night? I thought we could go to dinner and a movie."

Donna: "No thank you Frank. I like you as a friend, but I don't date coworkers. It's just too awkward if the relationship ends."

While the rejection may sting a bit, the reply is honest. If Donna makes an excuse instead, she'll find herself making excuses every weekend. Sometimes we need to deliver a "no" just as we'd remove a Band-Aid—with care, but quickly, so a painful situation isn't prolonged.

The same goes for the example below. If Lee wants to be honest with Martin about why he's not willing to help this weekend, it might be the best way to let Martin know that people will not be willing to help him if he's slacking off at work and expects others to help him catch up.

Martin: "I've fallen behind on my progress report. Any chance you can come in and give me a hand on Saturday?"

Lee: "Martin, I'm sorry you've fallen behind. But you said you spent four hours yesterday shopping for golf clubs online instead of finishing the report. I don't feel I should give up my time off to help you this weekend given the circumstances."

In the example above, Lee likely felt it was important to let Martin know that he's unwilling to help out if Martin is wasting time during the week. Unfortunately, many people avoid honest explanations because they fear the other person's reaction. Sometimes though, it's the only way the other person will understand why someone is not willing to help.

3. Say "no" and offer an alternative.

The third way to say "no" is to decline, and then offer an alternative or qualification. We can use this method when we want to help people but can't provide the exact help they've requested.

For example, if Martin hadn't wasted time, and Lee did want to help but wasn't available this weekend, the conversation might sound like this:

> **Martin:** "I've fallen behind on my progress report. Any chance you can come in and give me a hand on Saturday?"
>
> **Lee:** "I can't on Saturday because I'll be out of town all weekend, but I can stay late Friday evening or come in early Monday to help, if that will work."

Other examples of offering alternatives include:

> *"I can't help you right now, but if I finish my monthly report by three o'clock, I can help you then. Will that work?"*
>
> *"I have a dentist appointment today that I'd rather not reschedule because I have a broken tooth. Can I come in early tomorrow to do the work?"*
>
> *"Laura, I'm so sorry I can't go to your promotion party. Can I take you to lunch Friday to celebrate? I'm so happy for you!"*
>
> *"I'm sorry I can't stay for the meeting, but can I help you set up before I leave for the day?"*

Offering alternatives allows us to show our willingness to help while maintaining our personal integrity and commitments.

ACT on this chapter

Analyze: People have different reasons for their difficulty in saying "no." Write a list of your reasons and then really analyze them. You'll find that many of your reasons for avoiding "no" are not valid. You might also find that you've allowed your needs to be pushed aside in favor of others', and it's time to get your own needs met.

Communicate: Balance your needs with those of other people. If the scale leans in your favor, say "no" using one of the methods from this chapter. Remember, when you say "no" after considering both sides of the situation, you're doing yourself *and* the other person a favor. When we say "yes" to something we don't want to do or don't have time to do, it's unlikely we'll put forth our best effort.

Tips: Learning to say "no" can be a challenge for many people. To build your self-confidence and get practice saying "no," start safe. Don't test your new "no" skills on your most difficult coworker. Instead, begin in less-challenging situations, such as with a salesperson or in the grocery store check-out line. If you're in the express line and a stranger asks, "Can I go next? I'm in a hurry." You might say, "I'm sorry, not today. I'm in a hurry also." Finally, in situations where you're unsure about saying "yes" or "no," ask for time to think about the request. Say, "Let me check my schedule, and then I can let you know for sure. Can I call you at noon?" A statement like this helps you avoid being put "on the spot" and gives you time to review the request and make the best decision for both you and the other person.

Chapter 5

Checking Your Perceptions

PEOPLE are complex beings, and as such, have a lot of information to process as they move through their lives. Each day our senses are inundated with that information—some is important, some is useless. Our perception process helps us to organize and make sense of all of that data.

Human perception is a three-step process of selection, organization, and interpretation. We select certain things to pay attention to, organize what we've selected by categorizing it into logical groups, interpret and assign meaning to what we've seen or experienced, and then we move on to something else.

Selection

If six people were at a party, each would notice different things about it. Some would focus on the guests, some on the décor, and some on the food. Selection is the process we go through in noticing certain things in our environment. It's based on need, preconceived ideas, age, gender, and many other factors that make people different from each other.

Organization

Once we notice things, we try to make sense of them. Because our senses are bombarded by information on a daily basis—too much information to interpret individually—we lump experiences together to quickly interpret that information. We normally react based on those categorizations. "What is it?" "Where does it fit in my memory bank?"

Interpretation

Once we figure out what it is and make sense of it, then we attach meaning. "Is it good or bad?" "Is it fair or unfair?" "Do I like it or not?" Then either we move on to something new, or we might take action on what we've perceived.

We use this same process when trying to make sense of others' actions. We see someone do something or hear someone say something, and we create perceptions.

The problem with the human perception process is that people don't differentiate between their perceptions and reality. Additionally, people act or react based on their perceptions—which may or may not be accurate—and can often make situations worse.

For example, David is walking down the hallway at work and passes Claire. He says, "Hey, Claire! How are you?" Claire does not respond or react to what David says and simply continues walking.

So what does David do? He relates Claire's actions to previous, similar actions he's experienced in order to gain some perspective. In doing so, he's able to create several reasons, based on those previous experiences, as to why Claire didn't react to his greeting.

What does it mean when we say "hello" to someone and we don't get a reply or response?

- *The person is angry with us.*
- *The person doesn't like us.*
- *The person is rude.*
- *The person has laryngitis.*
- *The person is preoccupied.*
- *The person has earphones on and didn't hear us.*

Any of these possibilities could be the truth. Therefore, based on his own perceptual processing, David picks the interpretation that is most logical to him: "Claire must be angry with me about something."

Is his interpretation of Claire's actions correct? Who knows? Will David go find Claire and ask her if his interpretation is correct? Not likely. It's more likely that David will move forward and act on his interpretations.

If he's an aggressive person, he might confront Claire, "Hey, I said hello to you this morning, and it was pretty rude of you not to reply!"

If he's a passive-aggressive person, he might "return the favor" and make a point not to respond the next time Claire greets him.

If he's a more passive person, he may keep his thoughts and feelings to himself and never bring it up, or he may try hinting or asking questions, such as, "Is everything okay?" hoping to find out what's going on.

Instead of guessing or creating our own potentially incorrect interpretations of others' behaviors, we should seek clarification.

To check our perceptions, we should:

1. State the behavior we've observed using factual, nonjudgmental language.
2. Share our interpretations of the behavior, ideally giving two possible interpretations of that behavior— at least one should give a benefit of the doubt.
3. Request clarification from the other party.

David could very easily approach Claire later in the day to check his perceptions.

> **David:** "Claire, this morning when we passed in the hallway, I said hello, and you didn't respond. I thought you may not have heard me, but I also thought it was possible you were upset with me about something. Is everything okay?"

Taking the time to talk about his perceptions allows David to share what he's thinking and allows Claire to clarify the situation from her perspective.

Verifying perceptions helps us avoid misinterpreting others' actions so that we don't damage our relationships. It's also a great way to clear the air when the other party might not be willing to bring a problem to our attention. If Claire had been angry with David about something and he then shared his perceptions and interpretations, it's possible she would have told him why she was upset.

The key to verifying perceptions is using facts and nonjudgmental language to describe a person's behavior. If we don't, we're likely to get a defensive response. For instance, we should say, "This is the third time I received the report late," not, "You never turn anything in on time." The first statement is factual. People who turn in a report late for the third time, if they're being honest with themselves, know this to be true and would have a difficult time refuting it. The second statement is just a lead-in to an argument. Most people would be unlikely to agree that they never turn things in on time.

When providing interpretations of others' behavior, it's best to give them benefit of the doubt. Who would want to choose between, "Were you intentionally trying to embarrass me, or are you just a jerk?" However, there may be instances when it's important to express to people our honest, even negative, interpretations of their behaviors. If we do, we can still use our second interpretation to give benefit of the doubt. If we believe someone was intentionally trying to embarrass us, and we want the behavior to stop, we need to be honest. However, we should use the negative interpretation with caution and only when we have evidence to back it up.

> *"When you said in the staff meeting that you couldn't complete your report because I didn't e-mail you the statistics, at first I thought you might not have realized that comment would embarrass me. However, since I'd already asked you to bring problems like this to my attention privately before the meeting, I am starting to believe you intentionally want to embarrass me. Can we talk about it?"*

ACT on this chapter

Analyze: How many times in the past have you jumped to conclusions about others' actions and motives? When you did, what was the result? Did you stew with hurt feelings, lash out aggressively, or do something in-between? Remember that perceptions are only reality to the individual who is doing the perceiving. If several people experience the same thing, it's likely each will have different perceptions of the situation.

Communicate: Remember to think before you act on your perceptions. When you feel the urge to jump to conclusions in interpreting others' actions, verify your perceptions with them instead. You'll likely find that verifying your perceptions will help you clarify issues and concerns between yourself and others and your working relationships will benefit. You might also notice in time, the people around you won't be so quick to judge and instead, will reciprocate by coming to you to verify their perceptions of your behavior.

Tips: When verifying your perceptions with others, be sure to use factual terms to describe their actions. Also, when forming and sharing your interpretations, remember to consider alternative viewpoints and give benefit of the doubt whenever possible. Finally, in the spirit of honesty, when faced with a situation where you just can't come up with a positive interpretation, as a last resort, share your truth. People may not always be happy hearing your interpretations, but at least you get things out in the open—which might be the first step toward an improved relationship.

Chapter **6**

Paraphrasing to Ensure Understanding

IF we could read other people's minds, we would have a lot less miscommunication in the world. Knowing exactly what people wanted without them having to say a word would eliminate misunderstandings. However, since we can't read minds, we rely on others to paint pictures of their wants and needs using their words and nonverbal communication. Unfortunately, many people aren't good communicators, and as a result, the picture we end up with doesn't always resemble what they had in mind. Think about what most people say in response to others' comments and requests, "Uh huh," or "Okay, got it." How exactly do these phrases clarify to the speaker that we truly understand what's been said? When we don't do our part to confirm our understanding, we're just as much at fault for the unclear outcome.

Imagine looking at a picture of a house and trying to describe it to a group of artists so they could draw it exactly as it appears in the picture. What are the odds the artists' drawings would look the same if they did nothing to confirm the details we shared with them? Although some aspects might be similar—the existence of doors, windows, a roof—the finer details might be missing, such as scale, number of floors in the house, and the exact color, among other important details.

Imagine a vague description of the house mentioned above. The person describing the drawing may say the house has a door, two windows, and is the color of an apple. Paraphrasing that description can clear up any vagueness and allow for a more accurate final product.

Andy: "Just so I understand you—the house has one door, two windows, and is red like an apple?"

Meg: "You've got it all correct except the color. I was thinking of a green apple. The house is green."

If we want to ensure we really understand what someone has said, we need to confirm what we think we've heard. We should go into every conversation knowing that people don't clearly communicate, and we must confirm our understanding before we walk away. What exactly about "uh huh" confirms to the speaker that we've understood what he or she has said? Nothing. All it does is give the speaker a false sense that we understand and encourages him or her to continue.

Paraphrasing is a tool we can use to verify what we think another person has tried to communicate. It allows us to tell the speaker, "Before I walk away with incorrect information and do the wrong thing, here's what I think you're saying ... Am I correct? Am I missing something? Please fill in the blanks."

Just as the goal with the house drawing was to capture the image as accurately as possible, the goal in communication is to match our mental picture as closely as possible to that of the person trying to communicate with us. Paraphrasing allows us to fill in those little details that would otherwise be missing, making the communication incomplete.

Paraphrasing is relatively simple. It's taking our understanding of what someone is trying to tell us and reflecting it back to them in our own words. If we are correct, they will tell us so. If not, they'll repeat or elaborate to paint a clearer picture.

Rhonda: "I need you to call Steven Marks from Dynex. He's the lead on development for the promotional project. I know he has several other companies scheduled for demos this week, so I need you to confirm that we're on his calendar for eleven o'clock Friday morning for our demo. I don't want to drive all the way out there and find out that they're not ready or have another company scheduled at that time. I also need to know if he's bringing any of his vendors in, or if it will just be him and Rick. I just want to be prepared."

> **Kim:** "Okay, so just to confirm. I'm calling Steve Marks and confirming we're definitely on his calendar for a demo this Friday morning at eleven o'clock, and asking whether his vendors will be there."

Paraphrasing is not parroting. It is not necessary for Kim to repeat every word that Rhonda said. What is important is to confirm relevant points. The details about Steven's role in the project and the fact that other companies are scheduled for demonstrations are not what Rhonda needs Kim to take away from their conversation. The bottom line is that Kim needs to ensure the meeting is on and to find out if vendors are attending. Once Kim offers the previous paraphrase, Rhonda has the opportunity to confirm that Kim has grasped the key points or to correct the information. As a result, they're more likely to be on the same page than if Kim had just said to Rhonda, "Uh, huh, got it," or "Okay, I'll take care of it."

> **Rhonda:** "Thanks Kim. This project has been nothing but hassles and wasted time. It's not as if Dynex is around the corner. It's a two-hour drive each way! I want the business, but I'm getting tired of this whole project, and I don't want to waste a day in the car for nothing."

> **Kim:** "You're right. It's a long drive to Dynex, and I can certainly see why you wouldn't want to drive there unnecessarily. Let's see what Steven says. Hopefully, this will be the last presentation, and we can wrap up this project by the end of the month."

In this example, Kim focuses on paraphrasing the intent of the message Rhonda is trying to express, rather than focusing on capturing factual details, as was necessary in the previous example. Rhonda is obviously frustrated by the way the project has progressed and the possibility of a long trip that could turn out to be a waste of time. Kim's paraphrase lets Rhonda know she hears her frustration, and that she's sympathetic.

ACT on this chapter

Analyze: Take time to evaluate your listening skills. Are you really listening, or just waiting your turn to talk, all the while formulating what you're going to say, instead of processing what others are telling you? Have you done everything you can to ensure you're walking away with the correct picture, or are you just hoping for the best and saying, "uh huh"? If your listening skills need some improvement, paraphrasing is a great way to start.

Communicate: When you feel the urge to say "uh huh" while listening to someone, paraphrase instead, so you can confirm what you think you've heard. Not only will the accuracy of your communication improve, but people will appreciate your excellent listening skills, your willing-ness to ensure you've interpreted them correctly, and your ability to understand what they're really saying and feeling, even if they don't put it into words.

Tips: When paraphrasing, try to offer the most accurate interpretation of what you've heard as possible. Exaggerating, editorializing, or being inaccurate will turn your attempt at listening into an analysis of your paraphrase. For example, a friend says, "I can't believe my neighbor parked his car in front of my driveway; that's so rude." You wouldn't want to say, "What a jerk, I bet you felt like killing him!" Instead, stick to an accurate interpretation—not how you'd feel in that situation. A better response would be, "It must be frustrating to come home and not be able to get into your own driveway."

Chapter 7

Empathy

MANY people have heard that empathy is putting yourself in someone else's shoes. This is a simple way of saying that we should try to see things from the other person's perspective and try to understand how they feel—simple to say, but not as simple to do. Many of us try to be empathetic, but in doing so, we have a hard time getting out of our own shoes.

To empathize with another person means that for a moment we put aside our own feelings, values, and judgments, and try to take on those of the other person in order to we can understand their situation. To truly empathize, we need to listen to not only what people say with their words but also what they say with their facial expressions and body language—in other words, we need to read what they're feeling. Sometimes people express how they feel with words. Someone might say, "I'm angry that I wasn't selected for the promotion." However, in most instances, we have to listen to what the person's voice and body language are telling us. To express empathy to others, we need to tell them that we understand what their words and nonverbals are telling us.

For example, Tom walks into the room, his shoulders are slumped, and he lets out a heavy sigh. We say, "Is everything all right?" To which he responds, "I guess … I just heard that Carl got the account executive position I applied for."

What should we say next?

1. "That's great. I'll have to go congratulate him. He's perfect for that job."

2. "That's too bad, but I don't know why you wanted that job anyway. I would never have applied for it."

3. "I'm really sorry, but I'm sure you'll get the next AE job that opens up."

The answer is: none of the above. The first answer, although nice for Carl, completely ignores Tom's feelings about not getting the job. The second answer is common. In an attempt to make the person feel better about the job he didn't get, we make a negative comment about the job. The problem with this response is that Tom wanted that job or he wouldn't have applied for it. In our attempt to make Tom feel better, we're really sending the message, "You were stupid to apply for the job," and he may end up feeling even worse after talking with us. The third example is nice, apologetic, and positive. However, it doesn't acknowledge what Tom said or how he feels. A response like this can often come across as a "brush off" and uncaring.

An empathetic response paraphrases a person's words and feelings. It demonstrates we are really paying attention to what the other person is trying to communicate to us. It also lets the other person know that we're interested in listening to their thoughts and feelings about the issue. Although Tom never says, "Hey, I'm upset I didn't get the job. I really wanted it and I need to talk to someone about it. Do you have time to talk?" His comments and nonverbal communication indicate he wants to talk about it. Otherwise, he would have remained silent.

As we saw in the previous chapter, paraphrasing is a useful tool to confirm details and to show others we are really listening to them. Paraphrasing can also be used to show others we empathize with their thoughts and feelings. To express empathy, paraphrase the words the speaker has expressed, including any emotions he or she has stated.

If emotions were not stated but instead implied nonverbally, paraphrase those as well. When people use nonverbal methods to communicate, the nonverbal message is often more important than the words they said. Because some people are uncomfortable or unable to communicate their feelings verbally, acknowledging their nonverbal messages will make them feel truly understood.

Lynda: "Is everything all right?"

Tom: "I guess . . . I just heard that Carl got the account executive position I applied for."

Lynda: "You sound disappointed. I know you really wanted that position. Do you want to talk about it?"

When we try to empathize with others, we may not always "read" their feelings accurately, especially when they don't specifically state how they feel. However, even if we don't get it quite right, attempting to empathize shows that we're good listeners and are truly interested.

Lynda: "You sound disappointed. I know you really wanted that position. Do you want to talk about it?"

Tom: "I'm not disappointed. I'm just so surprised. I thought for sure I would get the job."

Empathizing isn't easy. It takes good listening skills, the ability to read nonverbals, and—the most difficult part of all—the ability to put aside our own thoughts and feelings about the situation. However, it is an essential tool for building great working and personal relationships. It is also one of the most important listening skills you can use to show others that you truly care about them.

ACT on this chapter

Analyze: How many times in the past few weeks has someone you know expressed a need for empathy? Most of the time, people don't open up and ask for it directly. A child comes home from school and slams down his or her books on the table. A coworker sits down at the desk next to us and lets out a heavy sigh. An employee jokingly remarks, "I sure hope I can get all this work done by tomorrow." All of these types of instances are opportunities to show others you're paying attention—that you "hear" their need for understanding.

Communicate: Empathy is one of the most important communication skills for building and improving business and personal relationships. People just want to be heard, and they want others to care. Show the people around you that you care by paying attention to what they're "really" trying to tell you. Take the time to listen and let them know you hear how they feel, even if they don't verbally express their feelings.

Tips: Showing empathy to another person is a tremendous gift that you can give. Remember that it's important to reflect back to the other person how you believe he or she feels—not how you would feel in that situation. It's important that you take off your own shoes and get into theirs. Just as paraphrasing, exaggerating, or editorializing can really take away from your empathetic efforts. Remember, with empathy, it's all about that person, not you.

Chapter 8

Expressing Your Emotions Appropriately

WHEN we were children and had little to no vocabulary, we only had one way to express our feelings—nonverbally. We cried, threw ourselves on the floor, and kicked our feet. Our parents interpreted our actions to mean that we felt something—anger, frustration, sadness, or all three. They reacted by picking us up, trying to distract us, comforting us, or using some other method to get the tantrum to stop. From this, we learned that people know how we feel by the way that we act. As a result, most of us go through our lives crying, throwing ourselves on the floor, and having tantrums to express our anger and frustration even though we've long since possessed the words to express ourselves. Those who do attempt to verbalize how they feel are usually just as non-productive. Sarcasm, name-calling, and hinting to express emotions are also unclear methods and are unlikely to get the desired response. Unless we communicate clearly about what's bothering us, how we feel about it, and what we want others to do about it, nothing is likely to change.

Nancy and Sandra are coworkers. Both are supposed to arrive at work by eight o'clock in the morning. They both work the switchboard for the first two hours of the day before moving on to their other duties. For the past few days, Nancy has arrived at work fifteen to twenty minutes late, leaving Sandra to answer all incoming calls by herself. Sandra has become increasingly frustrated and has tried to let Nancy know how she feels, but nothing has changed.

Sandra began "expressing her feelings" nonverbally by leaving the switchboard to take a long restroom break the minute Nancy arrived. She hoped Nancy would get the hint and wanted Nancy to experience how hard it was to manage calls alone. When that didn't work, she tried verbally hinting.

"Wow! I can't believe it's 8:20 already. It sure has been a busy morning! These phones have been ringing off the hook!" Although Nancy said she was sorry, she was still late to work the next day. Today, when Nancy walked in with a breakfast takeout bag, Sandra said, "Must be nice to have time to stop for breakfast." Sarcasm didn't do the trick either because Nancy just responded with a weak laugh and an offer to share her breakfast. Finally, Sandra had enough and this afternoon walked up to Nancy and let her have it. Well, she finally got a response from Nancy, but it wasn't the conversation she expected.

> **Sandra:** "You know what Nancy, I'm sick and tired of doing your work for you and covering for you with the boss because you can't manage to get here on time like the rest of us!"

> **Nancy:** "I can't believe you! I've covered for you so many times I've lost count. I thought we were friends, but apparently not. Besides, you've been late plenty of times, so you have no right to say anything to me. I'm done with this conversation!"

Why do people use behavior, hinting, sarcasm, and aggression when they could just be direct and tell the others how they feel? Because they don't know how to express their feelings appropriately in a direct, non-confrontational way.

Using an "I Language" statement allows us to communicate how we feel in a way that is clear, specific, and non-defensive. It's the best chance we have for letting others really know how we feel and for getting an appropriate response from them.

To deliver an effective "I Language" statement, we should:

1. Describe the other person's behavior.
2. Express our feelings about the behavior.
3. Explain the behavior's consequences for others or ourselves.
4. Make a request for future behavior.

1. Describe the other person's behavior.

When describing the person's behavior, be sure to specifically describe the behavior and leave out judgments and evaluations.

> *"You've been fifteen minutes late three times this week."* This statement is specific and factual—assuming you're telling the truth.

> *"You're a slacker and aren't doing your fair share."* This statement is nonspecific and judgmental.

When we're specific and nonjudgmental in describing people's behavior, it's difficult for them to argue or get defensive about something that's true. When we use nonspecific or judgmental language, the conversation is likely to deteriorate, because when judged, most people become angry and defensive.

2. Express our feelings about the behavior.

When expressing feelings, we should begin with, "I am …" or "I feel …" and not "You make me …" Taking responsibility for our feelings is also less likely to create a defensive response than blaming others for making us feel a certain way.

3. Explain the behavior's consequences for others or ourselves.

When explaining the consequences, note that there may be many different consequences. Those consequences might affect ourselves, the person we're confronting, the organization, our customers, or others.

It's important that people know the consequences of their behavior. Negative consequences can be a strong motivator for changing poor behavior. There may be instances in which a person's behavior has several consequences. We don't need to list them all, but we should be sure to list the ones that are most important or relevant to the situation.

4. Make a request for future behavior.

When making a request, be specific in describing the desired future behavior. In some instances, the request is implied. However, more often than not, we need to let people clearly know exactly what we need from them in the future. If the person already knew what was appropriate or what we needed, he or she would likely already be doing it. Sometimes we just need to spell it out.

> *"This is the third time this week you've been more than fifteen minutes late. (behavior) I am frustrated, (feelings) because I can't effectively answer your phone and mine—and the boss is getting complaints. (consequences) I need you to be here on time starting tomorrow." (request)*

> *"You've been fifteen minutes late three times this week. (behavior) I'm frustrated (feelings) about having to answer two phones, and I'm worried (feelings) that you're going to get into trouble with the boss. She came by today because she'd received some complaints. (consequences) I covered for you today, but I need you to be here at eight o'clock from now on because I can't continue to cover for you." (request)*

Notice that the examples illustrate different approaches but still clearly communicate the problem, how the speaker feels about the situation, and what will happen if the behavior continues. The second example includes two expressions of emotions, because there are times when we may have several emotions about a situation; we could be both angry with someone and worried about the consequences. We can reveal one or several emotions based on what we feel the other person needs to know.

Using "I Language" to assert our emotions can help in numerous interpersonal situations: from sending back a meal at a restaurant to communicating with a spouse; from dealing with a customer service provider over the phone to interacting with coworkers. Being specific about the problem, clearly expressing our own feelings, and calmly explaining the potential undesired results helps to create better communication and more ownership of a solution from both parties.

ACT on this chapter

Analyze: Think of the times you've felt sad, angry, or frustrated. If your feelings resulted from another person's actions, did you tell him or her how you felt? Most likely, you didn't, or if you did, an argument may have ensued. People have a right to express their feelings. However, if you want yours to be heard, how you express them can make the difference between building understanding with others or starting an argument.

Communicate: Instead of keeping your thoughts and feelings bottled up, hinting and hoping people "get it," using sarcasm, or getting to your boiling point and exploding, take the straightforward approach of an "I Language" statement. When delivered correctly, the result is usually changed behavior and improved communication with the other person. In fact, "I Language" often motivates others to reciprocate in sharing their feelings, which makes for a more positive working environment and better working relationships.

Tips: Being specific when describing behavior, both what you've observed and what you'd like to see in the future, is crucial to ensuring your feelings are "heard" by the other person. Take full responsibility for your feelings, being sure to say "I feel" or "I felt" and not "You made me feel ..." Finally, be sure you're expressing an actual emotion; sad, happy, hurt, embarrassed, and angry are emotions. "I feel like you don't like me" is not an emotion, but an interpretation. "I feel like punching you in the nose" also isn't an emotion. If you feel like punching someone in the nose, it's likely that you're angry, so say that instead.

Chapter 9

You're Right

N O two words are sweeter to the ear than, "You're right!"
Who likes to be wrong? No one.
How often do people tell us we're wrong or disagree with us?
Often.

To understand the power of "you're right," we need to start with the basic animal instinct of fight or flight. In the animal world, these are the only two options when confronted by an aggressor. When facing down a lion, a zebra doesn't have the option to stand on its hind legs, put its hooves on its hips and say, "Okay Leo, let's talk about this. You say you're hungry and I don't want to be your dinner. Can't we work this out?"

However, people are able to negotiate. Unfortunately, most of us don't learn effective communication and negotiation skills. Therefore, when confronted, instinct kicks in, and fight or flight often takes the form of defense or denial.

Because the defense/denial response is so common in confrontational conversations, many people begin interactions already expecting defense or denial as a response. Because they believe they're going to get a negative response, they often begin the conversation with a defense-inducing tone or approach. Just as a boxer puts his hands up in preparation for the fight before the round begins, people initiating a potentially confrontational conversation approach the interaction ready for a fight. When they hear "you're right," it brings down their defenses and opens up the possibility of a productive conversation.

Mark: "I got a call from Susan Davis this morning. She said she didn't get the proposal yet. I thought you were going to send it to her Tuesday?"

David: "I don't know why you left it to me to send it. You're the lead on this project. You should have sent it." (defensive response)

———————

Connie: "I thought you said you would be finished with the research by Wednesday."

Terry: "I never said I was going to be finished by Wednesday. I said I'd try to have it finished by Wednesday." (denial response)

———————

Customer: "I can't believe it's been six weeks and I still haven't received my refund. Obviously, you don't care about your customers."

George: "That's not true; we do care about our customers. It just takes a while to process refunds." (denial response)

None of these responses is likely to be the beginning of a positive conversation. In fact, when confronted with a question, problem, or complaint, immediately responding to the speaker defensively or with denial will likely lead to conflict.

The power of "you're right" lies in accepting responsibility, agreeing with facts, and acknowledging the speaker's beliefs or feelings. Let's see how these same statements sound when the response begins with "You're right."

> **Mark:** "I got a call from Susan Davis this morning. She said she didn't get the proposal yet. I thought you were going to send it to her Tuesday?"
>
> **David:** "You're right, I was going to send it Tuesday. I'm sorry, I forgot. I will send it right now, and then I'll give Susan a call to apologize."

In this example, David simply agrees with what's true. He told Mark he would send the proposal by a certain date but he didn't. In the previous example, David got defensive and tried to put the blame on Mark by saying that Mark should have sent the proposal. David should avoid this type of defensive response. If David felt that Mark should have sent the proposal himself, he should have said so to Mark initially instead of agreeing to send the proposal.

> **Connie:** "I thought you said you would be finished with the research by Wednesday.
>
> **Terry:** "You're right, and I did try to have it finished by Wednesday. However, I wanted to be sure that I included all the correct statistics so it took me a little longer. I'll have it done this afternoon."

In the example above, it would be easy to respond defensively, as in the previous example, and say, "I said I'd try to get it done. I never promised anything."

However, Connie obviously walked away from the initial conversation with the impression the work would be done by Wednesday. There's no point in quibbling over the word "try." It's best to simply acknowledge the speaker's interpretation and then state your understanding of the situation.

Customer: "I can't believe it's been six weeks, and I still haven't received my refund. Obviously, you don't care about your customers."

George: "I understand your frustration and you're right, six weeks can be a long time to wait. Maybe if I explain the refund process it will help."

In this customer service example, of course we wouldn't agree with the entire statement, "You're right, we don't care about our customers." What we want to agree with is the fact that it's logical for a customer to think six weeks is a long time and that the customer is obviously frustrated by the long wait. Therefore, we agree with—or at least acknowledge—the customer's frustration and the fact that six weeks is a long time. In other words, we agree with the parts of the conversation that are true and correct.

ACT on this chapter

Analyze: So many times we see others' challenges, complaints, and emotions as opportunities to share an alternate viewpoint, to tell them they're wrong, or to force upon them how they *should* see things. How many times in the past have you said, "Yes, but (insert your own opinion)" or "You've got it all wrong ..." Each time we do this, we're setting up a challenge, inviting the other person to "fight back" to make him or herself heard.

Communicate: When you feel the urge to disagree with people or defend your position, instead identify and acknowledge those things with which you can agree. Once you've agreed with something they've said, you can proceed to explain your position or express your concerns.

Tips: Especially when someone is complaining or upset, finding something with which to agree and stating so immediately in your response, really helps de-escalate the situation. Although you should not agree with some-thing that's not true—"You're right, I am a lazy jerk"—most complaints usually contain a truthful element or perception the person has with which you can agree. If you cannot find anything specific, you can simply say, "I can see how you might see it that way," without saying, "You are right."

Chapter *10*

If You Don't Know,
Find Out

LET'S face it, when we're in leadership or customer service positions, people expect us to have the answers. When we don't and make no effort to find out, at a minimum we look incompetent, and at most we look as if we don't care.

> **Customer:** "Where do I go to get my blood drawn?"
>
> **Employee:** "I dunno. Check on the third floor."

What do you mean you don't know? You work here.

> **Customer:** "What do I do if my check is put on hold?"
>
> **Employee:** "I don't know I'm just a teller. You'll have to check with bookkeeping."

But the switchboard transferred my call to you, and I was told you would help me.

> **Employee:** "Hey boss, do you know when the holiday shift schedule will be posted? I'd really like to plan my vacation. I haven't seen my mom in five years."
>
> **Supervisor:** "I don't know. Charlie is taking care of it."

Aren't you supposed to be in charge? Realistically, we can't possibly know everything. However, we need to demonstrate a willingness to find out. We can start by trying to avoid the phrase, "I don't know." No one cares what you don't know; what they care about is getting the information they need so help them get it.

Customer: "Where do I go to get my blood drawn?"

Employee: "Let me make a quick phone call to check. I'd hate to send you to the wrong floor."

———

Customer: "What do I do if my check is put on hold?"

Employee: "Let me check with bookkeeping; they know the procedures for check holds. Would you mind holding while I call them?"

———

Employee: "Hey boss, do you know when the holiday shift schedule will be posted? I'd really like to plan my vacation. I haven't seen my mom in five years."

Supervisor: "Charlie is working on the holiday schedule. I'm meeting with him in a few minutes. I'll ask him, and then let you know."

At minimum, if we're not able to find the answers to questions, we should point the person in the right direction.

Customer: "Where do I go to get my blood drawn?"

Employee: "If you walk over to the information desk over there, Lisa will be able to tell you. I'm new here and would hate to send you to the wrong floor."

———

Customer: "What do I do if my check is put on hold?"

Employee: "The people in the bookkeeping department know the procedures for check holds. Would you like their phone number, or would you like me to transfer your call?"

Employee: "Hey boss, do you know when the holiday shift schedule will be posted? I'd really like to plan my vacation. I haven't seen my mom in five years."

Supervisor: "Charlie is working on the holiday schedule. If you call him or send him an e-mail, I'm sure he'll be able to tell you when the schedule will be ready."

It's not to say that we should never say, "I don't know." Saying "I don't know" is an honest and acceptable response, as long as it's followed with "but I'll find out" or "but I know who does." All of the appropriate examples above could begin with "I don't know" and then continue with a satisfactory explanation of how the question will be answered. In some instances, however, we can project more confidence and competence saying something more than "I don't know."

ACT on this chapter

Analyze: How many times in the past few weeks have you taken the easy way out by telling someone "I don't know," instead of taking the initiative to help? It may have saved you time at that moment, but what did it cost in the long run? Consider how going the extra mile will affect future interactions with friends, family, and clients, and how much it is appreciated when that effort is returned.

Communicate: Remember: people won't care what you don't know as long as you show a willingness to help them. If you don't know the answer to a question, but know someone who does, take the initiative and check with that person. At the very least, point the questioner in the direction of someone who knows the answer or go the extra mile and find the answer yourself.

Tips: You can't be expected to know or remember everything, but if you frequently receive repeat questions or inquiries, keep a "cheat sheet" with the answers to commonly asked questions, phone numbers of those who do have the answers if you don't, and other key information. Any time you can help a customer or coworker on the spot, you save time for not only yourself and for that person, but also for the people you might have "passed the buck" to in the past.

Chapter 11

Here's What I CAN Do

MANY organizations talk about the importance of providing great customer service, but don't necessarily put the talk into action. We go to the store to return a defective item, and the clerk says, "You can't return this. Our policy states that we don't take returns after thirty days. You bought this thirty-one days ago." Alternatively, we call a restaurant to make a reservation and the hostess says, "We can't take a reservation unless your party is more than five people."

Saying "can't" sets up a roadblock for action and is usually a conversation-ender. What's the point in continuing a conversation about what we can't do for someone? In addition to being a roadblock and a waste of time, the word "can't" is an emotional trigger word for most people—they don't like to be denied. They want to get their way, so when someone tells them they can't do something, they get angry or upset.

Wouldn't it be better to focus on what we *can* do to help the person or fix the situation?

> **Customer:** "I need to return this blouse and get a refund. I bought it a month or so ago and it's been hanging in my closet. I took it out yesterday to wear it and noticed it has a tear in the sleeve."
>
> **Clerk:** "I'm very sorry the blouse had a tear. Here's what I can do: I can give you a store credit for the price of the blouse, or if you'd like to exchange it for another one, we have that same blouse on the rack over here on the left."

Doesn't this sound better than the alternative? "You can't have a refund. Our policy states no refunds after thirty days."

Customer: "I'd like to make a reservation for tonight for three people."

Hostess: "What we can do is call-ahead seating. If you call thirty minutes before you arrive, I'll take down your name and arrival time, and you'll get priority seating when you get here."

Again, the example above sounds better than saying, "We won't take your reservation because you don't have enough people."

The difference between the can and can't examples above may seem minimal to some people. They may think, "What's the difference? No matter how you say it, the customer seeking a refund isn't getting her money back and the customer who wants a reservation isn't getting one."

The emotional reaction is what separates the examples above. When people want something, they want to hear that they can have it. When they're told they can't have what they want, they get frustrated and sometimes angry. By sharing what they can have or what we can do for them, we provide options, alternatives, and forward momentum that at least takes them in the direction of their goals.

Using "can" instead of "can't" doesn't mean people will always be happy. Some people will continue to fight for what they really want instead of what we've offered as an alternative. However, remaining positive rather than countering with negative after negative, or "won't, don't, and can't," will help maintain the positive tone of the interaction and will usually help us come to some agreement.

ACT on this chapter

Analyze: For the rest of the day, keep a tally of how many times you say or write the word "can't." You'll be likely surprised at the number. Now multiply that by 365 and you'll see how many times you put up roadblocks to action. No wonder people get upset so often. Roadblocks are everywhere!

Communicate: Try removing the word "can't" from your conversations whenever possible. Rather than telling people what can't be done, reassess the situation in terms of what you or they can do to fix the problem. When you feel the urge to tell people you can't do something for them, stop and think about options and alternatives to help the person. Then rephrase your comment to tell them what you can do for them. You'll likely find that you're facing a lot less anger and resistance than if you had told them what you couldn't do.

Tips: Although it's unlikely you'll never use the word "can't" again, be sure you always take the time to try to think of alternatives, options, and choices. If you need time to think about what can be done, tell the other party, "I'm not sure what the best option is at this point. Can I get back with you at ten o'clock tomorrow morning? That will give me time to research this problem, and then we can discuss where we go from here."

Chapter *12*

I Don't Have to Do Anything!

"ALL we have to do in life is pay taxes and die." Despite the simplicity of the saying, in reality there are many things we end up having to do in life, whether we really want to or not.

When it comes to things we don't want to do, we generally don't go quietly. We passively or actively resist, question, argue, and sometimes get angry. Even if we don't open our mouths and say something, we're likely thinking, "I don't *have* to do anything! Just watch me!"

Whether speaking to a customer, an employee, or to our children, beginning with, "You'll have to …" "You must …" or "If you don't …" is just asking for a fight. In fact, presenting a challenge through demands will likely only get us a challenge in return.

> "*You'll have to* help Susan; she's new and doesn't know how we do things around here."

> "*You must* fill out this form before I can place your order."

> "*If you don't* clean your room, there's no way you're going to the movies."

The odds that the response to any of these phrases will be, "You're right. Thank you for pointing that out. I'll get right on it," are pretty slim. Even if the people with whom we're speaking do not say the following, they are likely thinking:

I don't care that she's new. Why should I help her? I'm too busy!

I don't have to fill out anything. I'll take my business elsewhere.

I'm not cleaning anything. I'll just climb out my bedroom window and go anyway.

A common mistake people make when they want to avoid resistance is to turn the instructions into a question. Questions are a valid option in some instances. Sometimes we even get lucky, and the person says, "Sure, no problem!" The dilemma comes when we don't get the "right" answer.

Supervisor: "Can you please help Susan learn to log on to the payroll system?"

Employee: "Sorry, I don't have time."

_____

Clerk: "Can you please fill out this form?"

Customer: "No thanks."

_____

Mother: "Will you please clean your room?"

Child: "I'm not really in a cleaning mood today—maybe next week."

_____

What will we do with responses like the ones above?

When there is no alternative or option, we shouldn't imply there is one by asking a question. If the employee must help Susan, the form must be filled out for the order to be placed, and the room must be cleaned before the child can go to the movies, we shouldn't ask a question, making the request optional.

To avoid outright resistance and increase the odds that people will willingly do what we ask, we should change the wording of our statements by beginning them with phrasing such as:

"If you …"

"Once you …"

"When you …"

instead of, "You'll have to …"

"If you can help Susan learn how to log on to the payroll system, I'd really appreciate it. I'm sure you remember what it's like to be new here; there's so much to learn."

"Once you fill out this short form, I'll have all the information I need to fill your order immediately."

"When you've cleaned your room, I'll be glad to take you to the movies. I know it's a lot of work, but since Grandma is coming this afternoon and staying in your room, we can't have things on the floor that she'll trip on."

Rephrasing the statement doesn't change the fact that the person needs to fill out the form, help the coworker, or clean his or her room. Rephrasing just makes the instructions less demanding and more palatable; it takes out the challenge and puts the control into the hands of the listener. Now it's the listener's choice to either do it or accept the consequences. That transfer of control is less likely to result in unnecessary friction.

That is not to say that everyone will willingly do what we ask if we simply avoid demanding phrases. People may still resist. However, any resistance we face should be less intense or less frequent.

Sometimes people will continue to resist because they just like to argue or flat out disagree with our request. More often though, people resist because they don't understand the rationale behind the request. That's why the examples above are not just rephrased, but also provide an explanation of why the speaker is making the request. Although not required, an explanation goes a long way toward reducing resistance and gaining compliance.

ACT on this chapter

Analyze: Try to identify all the ways you make demands, and note how others challenge you. Watch out for phrases such as:

"You'll have to ..."

"You must ..."

"You'll need to ..."

"You'd better ..." (or else)

"If you don't ..."

Communicate: When you feel the urge to say any of the above, rephrase your comments, and you'll increase the odds that the other party may willingly do what you ask. You should get very different reactions from others than you usually do.

Tips: To avoid unnecessary resistance, provide an explanation or rationale whenever possible. When people understand the "why" of things, it improves the chances that they will cooperate.

Chapter 13

I'm Sorry

THERE are two types of situations that occur in our daily interactions when we might need to say, "I'm sorry." If we make a mistake, and it negatively affects someone else, we should apologize for the mistake and for the negative impact. A second instance is when we feel sympathy for the other party, such as when a coworker is upset about a difficult customer interaction. We might say, "I'm sorry you had such a rough time with that guy."

Many people have difficulty saying, "I'm sorry," or "I apologize," especially in customer service situations. For example, a customer comes into a store to return a faulty product, loudly complaining about the inconvenience of having to come to the store. The customer service provider could easily say, "I'm sorry for the inconvenience." However, many balk at doing so, because they equate the words "I'm sorry" with acceptance of blame and do not recognize the second purpose, which is to show sympathy for the other person.

> **Funeral attendee:** "I'm sorry for your loss. Your grandmother was a kind woman."
>
> **Relative:** "Why are you sorry? You didn't kill her."

Does that interaction sound ridiculous? The point is, in addition to saying "I'm sorry" when we've done something wrong or made a mistake, it's just as appropriate for showing sympathy or understanding to someone who's in a difficult situation. When we can't change the situation, sometimes a simple expression of sympathy is enough to meet the needs of the speaker or to keep an angry person's displeasure from escalating—especially if we follow the "I'm sorry" with an empathic statement.

> *"I'm sorry. I know it must have been frustrating to drive all the way back here to return the toaster."*

Even when some people are willing to say, "I'm sorry," they make the mistake of not letting the apology stand on its own. They don't take responsibility for their actions, but instead try to push the blame onto something or someone else, including the person with whom they're speaking. Packaging an apology with blame or excuses defeats the purpose of apologizing.

> *"I'm sorry I missed the deadline, but you should have given me more time. There's no way anyone could have completed that assignment in that amount of time."*

> *"I'm sorry I was late this morning, but the construction on the freeway is a nightmare."*

> *"I am sorry about eating your sandwich from the fridge in the break room, but you should have put your name on it so people would know it was yours."*

All of the apologies above are half-hearted at best. Using the word "but" as part of a statement negates the words that come before it and focuses attention on the words that come after it. What we're really saying with statements like these is:

> *"I'm not really sorry because it's your fault that you didn't give me enough time to do the work."*

> *"It's not my fault. It's the fault of the construction I've known about for months, but still haven't taken the time to find another route around it."*

> *"I'm not sorry at all. In fact, you're going hungry because of your own stupidity. You should have been smarter and labeled your food. Then I would have had one less excuse for stealing your lunch when I knew darn well I didn't bring a sandwich today."*

If we want apologies to sound sincere, we need to stop pushing responsibility for our actions onto other people or outside circumstances and just say, "I'm sorry" or "I apologize."

Additionally, for situations such as those in the previous examples, where we're apologizing for missing a deadline we felt didn't give us enough time, we should have let the person assigning us the work know that it wasn't enough time before the project began, not after the fact. If we didn't know at the time we received the assignment, but realize at a later point that we can't get the work done, we should immediately go to the person and renegotiate the work or the deadline, not wait until the deadline has passed.

Sometimes an apology is all we have to offer someone else, especially if we can't fix a mistake or make the situation right. People at least want to know that we feel badly about it. An apology is effective in situations where we're at fault or feel great empathy.

> *"I'm sorry I missed the deadline. I should have told you sooner that I wasn't going to get the work done on time."*

> *"I'm sorry I was late. I know by not being here on time I left you with more than your share of work."*

> *"I'm sorry I ate your sandwich. I knew it wasn't mine, and I shouldn't have taken it."*

ACT on this chapter

Analyze: Think about your attitudes about saying "I'm sorry." Do you avoid saying it? If you do, is it because you have trouble admitting your mistakes or faults? Or maybe because you don't like to be blamed for things over which you have no control? Remember, although very appropriate when we're in the wrong, "I'm sorry" doesn't always equate to fault. In many instances, it is just an expression of sympathy—sympathy that may be exactly what the other person needs at that moment.

Communicate: When you're wrong, take your lumps as appropriate. If you do something, even by accident, that negatively affects someone else, say you're sorry. If someone is in need of sympathy, provide it.

Tips: To ensure your apology is perceived as sincere, remember it's not the words you say, as much as how they're said. You need to look and sound as if you truly are sympathetic in order for others to believe you. Additionally, to be sincere, "I'm sorry" can't be followed by a qualifier. That means you can't say, "I'm sorry ... but you should have ..." or "I'm sorry ... but it's not my fault." When you say "but" you erase the apology. Leave the buts out to show you're taking full responsibility. If an explanation is needed, follow the guidelines for providing explanations rather than excuses in Chapter 15.

Chapter 14

Admitting Mistakes

MANY people avoid admitting when they make a mistake for fear of looking stupid, incompetent, or because they think the revelation will result in conflict. However, if the mistake is big or noticeable enough, it's bound to come out and confrontation is likely.

When we make mistakes, we can choose to be proactive or reactive. When we avoid admitting a mistake, we're likely to get caught. When we do, we put ourselves in a position of reacting to someone else's accusations or questioning, which usually results in a defensive or angry response on our part. Additionally, trying to avoid or hide a mistake affects others' view of our competence, credibility, and honesty.

When we "get out in front" of a mistake—not waiting to be caught, but admitting it before anyone even finds out—we put ourselves in the position of being proactive and in control of that conversation.

People who admit their mistakes without being prompted to do so are seen as more confident, competent, and honest. Additionally, people who admit their flaws and imperfections are generally more trusted and liked. Everyone knows there are no perfect people. Pretending to be perfect by not admitting mistakes can lead to a loss of trust—not to mention friends—in the workplace.

Admitting a mistake may include the following:

- Taking responsibility for the mistake
- Explaining how the mistake happened
- Apologizing
- Sharing lessons learned about the mistake
- A plan to avoid the mistake in the future

Sam to his supervisor: "Travis, I messed up. When I put the supply order in the computer, I inadvertently entered 15 in the quantity field instead of 150. I called the supplier, but the order had already shipped, so I couldn't correct the mistake. I was able to put in a second order for the remaining parts, but they won't arrive until next Monday. I'm very sorry about this. I know now that I have to be a lot more careful in checking the numbers before I send the order. I've already created a checklist for verifying my orders before I send them so this doesn't happen again. Also, I've already spoken to Mark in the parts department to let him know when the additional parts will be here. He said it shouldn't affect completion of the Tri-Star contract."

Although this was probably a difficult discussion for Sam to initiate and while Travis might still be upset about the mistake, there's not much Travis can say to Sam regarding what he should have done or should do next time because Sam has already identified these things. Apologizing, identifying how the mistake has been fixed and assuring—and ensuring—that the mistake won't happen again leaves little room for legitimate rebuttal from the person who was wronged. Saying, "You should have told me" won't work because the other person has already admitted the mistake. Asking, "What are you going to do to make sure this doesn't happen again?" only applies if the other person has not already identified a plan. The wronged person can't say, "You should be more careful," because Sam has already made a commitment to be more careful.

Imagine how much more difficult the conversation would have been if Sam hadn't told his boss, and Travis found out later the incorrect number of parts had been ordered.

> **Travis:** "Sam, I just got word from the parts department that XYZ Supply really screwed up and sent 15 parts instead of 150. I'm on my way now to give them a call and tell them if they don't have the additional parts here today, I'm going to find another supplier."

> **Sam:** "Umm, uh, actually Travis, I've already spoken to them about it. As it turns out, I made a tiny mistake and ordered the wrong number of parts. You see …"

> **Travis:** "What? This is your fault, and you're just now telling me? Why didn't you tell me sooner? Did you even try to get the order fixed?"

> **Sam:** "Yes, I did. I'm doing my best, but I was in a hurry and …"

> **Travis:** "In a hurry? Well your sloppy work may cost us the Tri-Star contract if those parts don't get here ASAP."

Which conversation sounds preferable? Again, it's not that Sam's boss won't still be upset or angry about the mistake, but he'll be a lot less upset when he realizes Sam has been very proactive in fixing the problem, rather than trying to hide it.

ACT on this chapter

Analyze: Think about a time when you made a mistake and tried to hide it or avoided admitting it, and you got caught. How did that feel? How did that incident affect the trust between you and the person who caught you? Although admitting mistakes is difficult, remind yourself that everyone makes mistakes, and every mistake is an opportunity to learn and grow. This mindset will help you admit your mistake and move on.

Communicate: When you make a mistake, make a point to admit it. Sometimes our mistakes are so small or insignificant they're not worth admitting. So don't feel the need to share everything. No one will be worried that you missed a free throw to the trashcan and had to go pick up the piece of paper. No one will be worried that you left something in the car and had to go back to the parking lot to get it. Focus on mistakes that have an impact on someone else—your boss, coworkers, or family—and get out in front of them rather than waiting to be caught. You'll feel a lot better about it when you do.

Tips: Remember, it's better to be the person proactively admitting mistakes than the person caught in a mistake who's forced to defend himself. If you make a mistake, let the appropriate people know immediately. If a key person is at first unreachable, keep calling, dropping by, or even e-mailing or text-messaging him or her. Saying "I dropped by your office two days ago to tell you about it, but you weren't in" is unlikely to alleviate the situation for a person who just found out about the mistake today.

Chapter 15

Explanations, Not Excuses

THERE are times when things go wrong, or when we know we can't undo what's been done, but we just want to know, "Why?"

Why is it taking so long for Angie to get me the graphics she promised?

Why didn't Paula call if she knew she was going to be late?

Why is the wait so long at this restaurant?

We just want some rationale, clarification, or details—in other words, an explanation. In many instances, we're annoyed because instead of explanations, we receive excuses.

If you look up the words "explanation" and "excuse" in the dictionary, at first glance they appear quite similar. Upon closer inspection, there is often a more negative definition associated with "excuse" that doesn't appear for "explanation."

Explanation: clarification, reason, details, an account of …

Excuse: justification, defense, to try to remove blame from …

When people interact, the difference becomes more obvious. Explanations are generally offered as fact—as clarification of why something occurred or is the way it is. An explanation is often unsolicited and offered proactively. Another example of an explanation is someone who offers one while taking full responsibility for his or her role in the situation.

The main difference between an excuse and an explanation is accountability. Generally, two types of situations have the potential for turning an explanation into an excuse:

1. When the explanation involves placing blame on someone else, especially when that someone is not around to defend him or herself *or* when we avoid responsibility by blaming the speaker.
2. When the explanation *only* comes after a complaint is made by another party, especially when we could have offered an explanation beforehand.

Eric: "It's three o'clock, and I still haven't gotten Mr. Smith's tax paperwork. You promised you'd have it to me by noon."

Karen: "I know I promised, and I tried to get it done. If you had let me know sooner that you needed it by Friday, I might have been able to do it. But I just didn't have enough time. I probably won't have it done until Tuesday."

———

Bob: "I thought this was a team decision. You took our input, and then we find out today from the graphics department that we're outsourcing the project. They've known about it for a week. Why are we the last to find out?"

Supervisor: "I didn't have any choice. I backed your plan to upper management, but they wouldn't go for it. They're the ones who wanted to outsource the graphics to save money."

———

Customer: "I was told by one of your employees, Larry, that I would receive my order no later than Wednesday. Well, it's now Friday, and I still haven't received it."

Supplier: "I'm really sorry about that. Larry is new here, so he probably doesn't know all the procedures. There's no way you would have received it by Friday because it takes four business days to process orders.

In these examples, even if the answers are truthful, they still come across to the listener as excuses.

Karen blames Eric for not giving her enough time to complete the paperwork rather than taking responsibility for the delay. If she knew it was unlikely that she would be able to get the tax paperwork ready by the deadline, she should have told Eric when he gave her the deadline. Even if she thought she could get it done, but then discovered as she got started that she wasn't going to make the Friday deadline, she should have gone to Eric rather than allowing the deadline to pass.

The supervisor blames upper management for making the decision, rather than taking any responsibility or providing a more detailed explanation of upper management's decision.

The supplier shouldn't throw Larry under the bus, regardless of whether he's new. The supplier should have simply explained the normal processing time and apologized for the miscommunication. He or she should also have followed up with Larry to ensure he had the correct information so the error wouldn't happen again.

As we saw in Chapter 14, when we admit a mistake up front, we're being proactive and can maintain better control of the conversation. The same is true when we deliver an explanation even though we haven't made a mistake. This might occur, for example, when we're explaining our own or others' rationale, decisions, and actions, so someone can understand the choices that were made.

Karen: "I wanted to let you know that I won't have Mr. Smith's tax paperwork ready for you by Friday like I promised. I'd like to explain why."

———————

Supervisor: "I just got back from my meeting with upper management, and I wanted to let everyone know the results. After researching all the options, they decided to outsource the graphics for this project. I know some of you will be disappointed. I would like to explain why they're outsourcing the graphics, so you'll better understand the company's position."

Even in a situation when you're not in the proactive position but responding to an inquiry or complaint, the way that you offer rationale can make the difference between the rationale being perceived as an explanation or an excuse.

Customer: "I was told I would receive my order no later than Wednesday. Well, it's Friday, and I still haven't received my order."

Supplier: "I can understand that you'd be upset, and I apologize. I can explain why you haven't received your order. You see ..."

Although people won't always love your answer, at least they'll understand the situation and will be less likely to escalate their complaint if they hear explanations instead of excuses.

ACT on this chapter

Analyze: Listen to others' conversations, watch the news, or read the newspaper and you'll see that people are full of excuses. Whether they're blaming others, the weather, or supernatural forces, there are many people out there who just don't take responsibility. Are you one of those people? If you are, it's time to start taking responsibility and when necessary, offering explanations not excuses.

Communicate: Focus on providing explanations that allow others to understand your rationale. If you know your actions or a situation within your control will cause others to wonder why an action was taken, provide an explanation up front. Be cautious that your explanations don't turn into excuses by blaming others as a way to avoid responsibility.

Tips: Remember, the main difference between an excuse and an explanation is accountability. Be sure when offering an explanation that you do so proactively. Offer the explanation up front; don't make the other person drag it out of you. Customers especially shouldn't have to say, "Why did that happen?" You should be prepared to explain before they have to ask the question. Finally, be sure you don't place blame on other people, especially if they aren't available to explain their actions. Simply focus on correcting the problem and then contact the person later to see what you can do together to avoid the problem in the future.

Chapter *16*

Acknowledging Good Work

THE word "feedback" has taken on a negative connotation for many people, perhaps because when we tally up the feedback in our lives, most of it has been negative. Because good performance is expected, people rarely acknowledge it. We expect to be seated at the restaurant within a few minutes, so when the hostess seats us quickly, we don't take the time to let her know we appreciate her speedy service. However, if she says the wait will be ten minutes, and it turns out to be eleven, twelve, or more, many people would be sure to let her know that her service is poor.

As we move through our daily lives doing what we're supposed to—and going beyond what's expected—few seem to notice or acknowledge it. Occasionally, someone might say, "good job," but not much more than that. Because of a lack of positive feedback, many people drop their level of performance, thinking, "Why should I try so hard to do my best when no one seems to care?" When the performance drops, *that's* when they'll finally get some feedback.

> *"What's wrong Jack? You used to turn in your work early, now I'm barely getting it on time. You need to step it up."*

> *"Billy, you used to be so quick with your deliveries. Now it's taking you half the day to make a handful. You'd better do a better job, or I'll need to find someone else who's more efficient."*

Finally, someone has noticed us—however, not in the way that we want. So we'll step up our performance a little, but in most instances, just enough to end the negative feedback. Rarely will someone go back to his or her former "110 percent effort."

If we want others to maintain a high work standard every day, we must acknowledge their good work immediately by offering positive feedback.

> **Positive feedback can be as simple as a two-part statement:**
>
> 1. A specific description of the person's positive performance
> 2. A description of the positive outcome of the performance

1. A specific description of the person's positive performance

It's not enough to say, "Good job, David," or "Keep up the good work, Lisa." It's important to tell the person exactly what he or she has done well for two reasons. First, it adds sincerity to the message. By being able to state exactly what the person has done, we show them that we're paying attention and we care about what they're doing. Second, it identifies the exact behavior they should repeat in the future, so there's no doubt what should be said or done the next time.

2. A description of the positive outcome of the performance

People need to know their actions have consequences for themselves, others, and for the organization. In the case of positive feedback, the consequences are, of course, positive. By conveying the positive consequences of someone's actions, we emphasize their importance and make it clear that all things, even the little things, matter.

> *"Ron, I want you to know you do a great job writing up the meeting minutes. You include just the right level of detail and get them e-mailed to everyone so quickly. It really helps us keep track of discussions and agreements from the meeting.*

> *Getting the minutes out so quickly also gives everyone plenty of time to review their action items so they'll know what they need to have done before the next meeting."*

> *"Theresa, you did a great job setting up and promoting the health fair. I know it took you several weeks, and you did a lot of the work on your personal time to ensure the event was successful. Your hard work really paid off. Tony from employee wellness said we had a record attendance this year that he attributes to your hard work setting up the event and the great job you did advertising the program."*

If we want to add icing to the cake, after providing the positive feedback, we can give the person time to talk about themselves and their accomplishments. People love to have the stage to share their successes.

> *"Kevin, I like the way you handled that angry customer. You kept your cool, spoke in a calm tone, answered all her questions, and gave her some great options to fix the problem. She was so angry before you started talking to her, but by the end, she was calm and walked away happy. Where did you learn to handle upset customers so well?"*

> *"Missy, this spreadsheet you created for the budget is excellent. It's so thorough and easy to read that I'm sure the budget meeting will take half the time we expected because of your hard work. Tell me how you went about creating it. I'm interested because I never would have thought of approaching it as you did."*

If we read these positive feedback statements aloud, we'd find that they take no more than thirty seconds to say. What a great investment of time—thirty seconds to make someone's day by letting him know he's doing a great job and to solidify in that person's mind what exactly is expected in the future.

Supervisors and managers should set a goal to provide positive feedback regularly to their employees. In fact, many supervisors keep a feedback journal, or even a simple spreadsheet to track the positive, negative, and lack of feedback given to their employees. If we all did, we'd likely find we're spending more time providing negative feedback than positive feedback, if any at all, to those who are doing well.

Keep in mind that positive feedback isn't just a *supervisor's* responsibility. No matter what role we play—boss, employee, coworker, customer, or parent—we should all take the time to let others know when they've done a great job and had a positive impact.

Finally, for positive feedback to be effective, it should meet the following criteria:

1. *It should specifically identify the person's actions and the outcome of those actions.*

In the previous examples, the people's actions are specifically outlined, so they'll have no trouble knowing exactly what they did correctly. They can do the same thing next time.

2. *It must be delivered sincerely.*

Even positive feedback filled with the most flattering prose can be ruined if delivered insincerely. Therefore, it's important that our nonverbals—facial expressions, body language, and tone—convey our positive feelings about what the person has done.

3. *It should be delivered face-to-face for maximum effectiveness.*

A face-to-face conversation allows us to use nonverbal communication to reinforce the sincerity of our comments. There is nothing more re-affirming than to have someone take time from her day, come see him in person, and tell him that he's done a great job. A follow-up e-mail is also effective at giving people actual evidence they can use for their performance appraisals.

4. It should be delivered immediately to reinforce the good behavior.

When people receive immediate positive feedback, they make the direct and immediate connection between the good work and the "reward" of good feedback. The further after the event, the less likely they will remember their actions and make those connections. Waiting to put a nice comment on a performance review six months after the fact is not only too late to keep the good work going, but may result in a decline in performance because the person may have felt unappreciated.

Although in most instances it's appropriate to provide positive feedback immediately, even publicly, there may be times when you might want to wait until later that day or as late as the next day to provide the feedback privately so as not to embarrass the person or make others feel they're insignificant.

ACT on this chapter

Analyze: If you look for it, you will see all kinds of "good work" happening all around you. The employee who comes in early, the coworker who handles an angry customer with finesse, even the child who does his or her homework correctly. There are dozens of opportunities each day to provide positive feedback, without being asked, to the people in your life.

Communicate: In the coming weeks, take the time to acknowledge the hard work and good performance of those around you. Don't take it for granted. It doesn't matter whether the performance is exceptional or nothing more than the job description states. All good work is worthy of recognition. Don't forget to provide positive feedback outside of work as well. Family members, neighbors, store clerks, and others need positive feedback just like everyone else.

Tips: It only takes a few seconds to make someone's day with positive feedback. Remember the ways to deliver the most effective feedback—face-to-face, promptly, and sincerely—and watch your positive relationships, as well as productivity, grow. If you are a supervisor, team leader, parent, or someone else who is in a position of authority over others, it is important that you track your positive feedback, so you will know if you are giving those around you the encouragement they need to keep excelling.

Chapter 17

Avoiding the Gossip Grapevine

GOSSIP is one of the many things that can lower workplace productivity. It also creates an environment of mistrust and can damage working relationships. Even if we don't start the gossip, listening to it, passing it on, or standing idly by while it's happening, makes us part of the gossip and helps perpetuate it.

Many people think those who gossip are focused on the person about whom they're gossiping. In reality, the act of gossiping is more about the act itself than the subject of the gossip.

People gossip for many reasons, including:

- *To vent.*
- *To feel better about themselves.*
- *To get even.*
- *To "build camps" or create alliances.*

Sometimes it's easy to identify gossip. Other times we may be participating and not even realize we are gossiping. It is helpful to define gossip, so we know what it is when we hear it.

On a basic level, gossip is *anything* discussed about another person, positive or negative, that the person has not given consent to the speaker to share with others.

Discussing with coworkers that we overheard the boss say Susie is being considered for a promotion is just as much gossip as if we discussed her impending layoff, that she's going through a divorce, or that another coworker doesn't like her.

It's not easy to avoid the gossip that flows around us, but there are several steps we can take to avoid gossip in the workplace:

1. Don't start gossip.
2. Don't be drawn into a gossip discussion.
3. Change the subject when gossip begins.
4. Disagree with the gossip and share alternative or more positive views.
5. Confront gossip perpetuators.

1. Don't start gossip.

No matter how tempting it may be to share a bit of "news" we've overheard or been told, we must keep it to ourselves. If approached and asked whether we know something, it's best to direct the questioner back to the subject of the information.

For example, Karen told her coworker Louis that she was getting a promotion. Darla, knowing that Karen and Louis are friends, approaches Louis.

> **Darla:** "Hey, you're friends with Karen; has she said anything about whether she got the promotion?"

> **Louis:** "You should check with her. If she has any news she wants to share, I'm sure she'll let you know."

Notice Louis doesn't lie by telling Darla he doesn't know anything, nor does he hint that he knows something—which often invites further questioning and cajoling. He simply refers Darla back to the best source for the information, the person who could answer her question.

2. Don't be drawn into a gossip discussion.

Even if we didn't start the discussion, simply being part of a discussion is being part of the gossip and keeps the gossip going.

Derek: "Hey, I heard from Maria that Tanya is pregnant. Isn't that great! Maria said Tanya and her husband have been trying to have a baby for more than a year. I remember when my wife and I had our first baby, I ..."

Candace: "I'm sorry Derek, I don't mean to interrupt, but I don't feel comfortable discussing Tanya's personal life. I'm sure if Tanya has something she wants to share, she'll tell us all when she's ready."

In some instances, the lines between gossip and empathizing with someone, or acting as a sounding board, can be blurred. If a coworker is having trouble with another coworker and comes to us to talk about it, it's acceptable to empathize with the coworker, as long as we don't add our "two cents" worth. We should also keep our comments short and then quickly recommend that the coworker discuss the issue with the person about whom he or she is speaking.

Kelsey: "Can you believe that Andy made me look like such a fool in the meeting? He never lets people speak without interrupting and contradicting them. He's such a jerk—always trying to make others look stupid so he can look good to the boss."

Amanda: "I can see you're upset, and I know how frustrating it is to be interrupted. I think you should talk with Andy about it. People don't usually change their behavior unless someone brings it to their attention."

Even if Amanda agrees with Kelsey and dislikes Andy too, she should avoid sharing her own feelings about Andy. If Amanda also has a problem with Andy, then she should follow her own advice and talk directly with him rather than jumping on Kelsey's bandwagon. If she shares her feelings with Kelsey, it will only continue the gossip conversation. Additionally, Kelsey may go back to Andy and say, "... and Amanda feels the same way too!" In that case, Amanda may be dragged into the situation.

3. Change the subject when gossip begins.

Although not an assertive method for addressing gossip, changing the subject can be a good way to stop it quickly and move on to something else. Sometimes people will get the "hint" that we don't want to be part of gossip and will discontinue it. It's also an acceptable option when we want to stop gossip in a group setting without directly confronting the person gossiping, so as not to cause conflict in front of others.

The problem with changing the subject is that it doesn't clearly let the people who gossip know that we disagree with their actions. It's also unlikely to keep them from gossiping again in the future. Therefore, even if you do change the subject, it's a good idea to talk with the target about your concerns when you can speak with him or her privately.

> **Yolanda:** "Can you believe how bad Mike's presentation was? He must have said, 'uh' and 'um' a hundred times! And, did you see how much he was sweating? I thought he was going to drown."

> **Keith:** "Okay, enough about this morning's presentation. Let's get the meeting started. The first agenda item is ..."

If changing the subject doesn't work, we can always remind Yolanda that if she has some feedback for Mike, it would be best to talk directly with him.

4. Disagree with the gossip and share alternative or more positive views.

Most people who gossip are looking for someone who will agree with them. When they come across someone who contradicts their viewpoint, the conversation generally comes to a halt.

Sharon: "I really can't stand that new girl Fiona. She's such a know-it-all. All she ever talks about is, 'At my last job we did this. At my last job we did that.' Maybe she should go back to her last job."

Robert: "I don't find her to be a know-it-all type at all. The few times she's offered ideas from her last job, I've found them to be really helpful."

Robert can also follow up by referring Sharon back to Fiona to discuss how she feels.

Linda: "I can't believe David thinks that idea of his is going to work. Does he really think our clients are going to accept the cost increases without a fight?"

Andy: "I think his idea is the only option. If we don't raise prices, I'm afraid we'll be out of business within six months. What do you think we should do instead?"

5. Confront gossip perpetuators.

Sometimes we may feel that if we're not directly involved in gossip and are simply overhearing it, we should just stay out of it. It's not our conversation after all. However, staying silent does nothing to stop gossip. Additionally, if people know we're within earshot, or the subject of the gossip finds out later that we were in the room, we could be perceived to agree with what was said, or at minimum, that we don't care about stopping the gossip.

In a situation where we hear a group of people gossiping, one option would be to walk over to the group and say, "I couldn't help overhearing you talk about Mindy. I think if you have a problem with the new schedule, you should let her know. That way she at least has the option to make changes if she needs to before it gets published."

Keep in mind, doing the right thing isn't always the same as doing the popular thing. An alternative would be to wait until one of the "key players" in the gossip group is alone later, and confront him or her using one of the previously mentioned methods.

Confronting gossip perpetuators also works when you find out they're gossiping about you. Although it's rare for people who gossip to admit it, the confrontation itself is often enough to stop the gossip.

> **Mindy:** "Elise, can we talk for a minute in the conference room?" (Then once in the conference room) "I'm concerned because of some of the things I've been hearing—that you might have a problem with my new scheduling plan. I would hope that if you did, you'd come to me and not others to discuss it."
>
> **Elise:** "I don't know what you're talking about!"
>
> **Mindy:** "Okay, well maybe I just misunderstood. Now that we've talked though, if you do have any concerns, or something comes up, I hope you'll agree to come directly to me. I want everyone's input so that the schedule will be successful. If I get it quickly and directly, it's a lot easier for me to make any necessary changes and address people's concerns."

At this point, it's possible that Elise will admit her concerns. Otherwise, she'll just say, "Okay," and hope Mindy drops the subject.

When we confront a gossip, we let him or her know that we won't sit by and allow it to happen. As previously mentioned, the discomfort of being confronted is enough to make many people stop gossiping. However, by staying calm and asking if they want to share their thoughts, we also send the message that we're open to honest feedback and are interested in hearing people's opinions—if they just bring them to us directly. This approach often helps those who "gossip" out of fear of direct confrontation, feel more comfortable with direct interaction in the future.

Avoiding gossip can be difficult and sometimes uncomfortable. However, when used consistently, the steps above will keep us out of the gossip loop and can sometimes help begin the process of stopping office gossip altogether.

ACT on this chapter

Analyze: It's unlikely there's anyone reading this book who has never gossiped. For many of us, it can seem like fun to keep up with the "news" about what's going on around us. Think about the people you tend to gossip about and what situations or circumstances get your gossip tongue wagging. The first step in correcting a problem is to identify it.

Communicate: Challenge yourself not to share information about others that they've not directly asked you to share. When others try to draw you into gossip, empathize with them if they're upset, but direct them to share their feelings with the person who can help them—the subject of the gossip.

Tips: If you're having trouble fighting gossip in your work-place, community organization, or in other groups, try avoiding common gossip locations and situations. For example, stay out of the break room if people tend to linger to gossip. As soon as that homeowner's association meeting is over, leave the meeting if people tend to stick around to gossip. Although stopping gossip is the right thing to do in most instances, sometimes one person can't stop it on his or her own. Sometimes, when you can't beat 'em, it's best to just walk away.

Chapter 18

Honesty is the Best Policy

ALTHOUGH many people say, "Honesty is the best policy," when it comes to communicating with coworkers, bosses, friends, and family, many of us find it easier to be dishonest— telling "white lies," or outright lies that make our own lives easier. Why would we tell people the truth when the truth might cause them to feel bad or start a conflict?

> **Mike:** "What did you think of my presentation?"
> **Susan:** "Uh, yeah, it was great." (She actually believes it was terrible.)

See how easy that is? The lie makes Mike feel good and avoids the potential conflict that may result if Susan were to tell him that she thinks he did a terrible job. Unfortunately, whether we tell a "little white lie," or a downright whopper, there are many negative consequences to dishonesty:

- We have to struggle to keep track of the lies we've told.
- The people we lie to continue behavior that may negatively affect them.
- Lies between two people weaken working and personal relationships.
- If the people we lie to find out the truth from someone else, they'll no longer trust us.
- Plain and simple: it's being dishonest.

So if honesty truly is the best policy, how can we be honest while avoiding potential hurt feelings and conflict? The quick answer is: we can't. There's no guarantee that being honest, and doing so as gently as we can, will help avoid hurt feelings or conflict. However, approaching honest communication the right way and at the right time minimizes the chances of negative consequences and allows everyone involved to reap the benefits of the truth.

First, consider when it's appropriate to be honest. Just because we believe something to be true, doesn't mean the other person needs to know it. For example, a coworker has a picture of his child on his desk. We think the child is too fat or too thin. Do we need to share that unsolicited opinion just because we honestly believe it? No. In general, it's best to offer our honest opinion when we find ourselves in one of the following circumstances:

- When someone has specifically asked for our input
- When someone would be harmed if he or she did not have the information
- When someone would learn, grow, be more productive, or become a better person for having the information

Provide others with honest input using one or more of the following guidelines:

1. Provide "positive honesty" in public, "negative honesty" in private.
2. Be specific and choose the "best" words to convey what you honestly think.
3. Balance "negative" honesty with sincere compliments.
4. Acknowledge previous successes.
5. When possible, avoid focusing on past mistakes or things that can't be undone, and instead, focus on what could be done better in the future.

1. Provide "positive honesty" in public, "negative honesty" in private.

In the previous example, if in fact Susan thought Mike did a great job, she should tell him on the spot. Because in this case she thinks he did poorly, she should save her comments for when she can provide them in private. To respond to his question, she might say, "I really haven't had time to digest all the information. Can I get with you later to let you know my thoughts?" This statement not only gets Susan out of the situation of lying (or telling the truth) in front of others, but is also honest because it's unlikely she would have meaningful feedback or suggestions immediately following his presentation.

2. Be specific and choose the "best" words to convey what you honestly think.

There's honesty and then there's brutal honesty. Susan needs to provide Mike with her evaluation of his presentation, but she certainly doesn't need to say, "That was the worst presentation I've ever sat through. It was torture. I couldn't understand half of what you said, and I think most of the audience was asleep."

The best way to provide honest input is to focus on specific things that need to be changed or improved and by choosing the kindest, most non-defensive words to express yourself.

Instead of: "Your presentation was way off base!"
Say: "The presentation included technical language that some people may not understand."

Instead of: "That's a really bad idea!"
Say: "I have some concerns about the idea."

Instead of: "You're completely wrong about that ..."
Say: "I disagree. I think we should ..."

Instead of: "You shouldn't wear that suit. It's ugly."
Say: "I think your blue suit would be better because it makes you look more authoritative."

Notice the details that differentiate the more sensitive examples from the ones preceding them. Accusatory words that would personalize the criticism are avoided. Avoid saying "you" or "your" to keep feedback from getting personal. Avoid labeling an idea as "bad." Express concerns and state your disagreement rather than telling people they're wrong.

3. Balance "negative" honesty with sincere compliments.

It's unlikely that someone's presentation, interaction with a customer, attire, or idea is *all* bad. Giving credit for the positive elements helps soften the blow or balance out the negative elements. Giving credit for positive elements is also a good way to acknowledge the good aspects before expressing concerns. It avoids appearing as if we're only focusing on the negative.

> **Mike:** "That presentation went like clockwork. I felt great—I was so comfortable with my material that I wasn't nervous at all. How did you think it went?"
>
> **Susan:** "I agree. You looked relaxed, comfortable, and very professional. Would you be open to a suggestion that may make your presentations even better?"
>
> **Mike:** "Sure."
>
> **Susan:** "Because most of your audience was made up of non-technical people, it might be a good idea to minimize the technical language and use as many everyday terms as possible. That way everyone understands and benefits from the information you present."
>
> ――――――
>
> **Darlene:** "I love this dress. Do you think it would be a good one to wear to meet the new client on Monday?"
>
> **Margaret:** "I do like the color of that dress; it's a great color on you. Because it's a first meeting though, I think a suit would

make the best first impression. Why don't you wear that navy blue suit you wore to the luncheon last month? It would be perfect."

Trisha: "So what does everyone think about my idea?"

Bob: "I think it's creative. I never would have thought of that option. I have concerns about the cost though. Have you researched the start-up costs for going in that direction?"

4. Acknowledge previous successes.

This is especially important when someone usually does a good job, but for some reason things went wrong this time. It's important to let him know that we realize this situation wasn't the norm.

Susan: "Your previous presentations were great, with just the right amount of technical language. In this one, I think there was a bit too much technical language."

5. When possible, avoid focusing on past mistakes or things that can't be undone. Instead, focus on what could be done better in the future.

In some cases, there's no need to dwell on what went wrong. The situation is over, and we can't rewind the clock and get a "do-over." It's a better use of everyone's time to provide people with suggestions for the next time they find themselves in a similar situation. Rather than telling Mike all the things that she didn't like about his presentation that is now over, Susan could say, "For your next presentation, I would review your content for technical terminology to see if there are everyday terms you can use instead. By using everyday terms, you ensure everyone in your audience understands your presentation—not just those who are tech-savvy."

ACT on this chapter

Analyze: Look back over the past few days or weeks and identify the little "untruths" you've told at work, at home, at the store, and other places. Although lies, little or big, may be easiest, they chip away at our integrity if we make them common practice.

Communicate: Make honesty your policy. Instead of lying to avoid conflict, or telling little white lies that really don't benefit the other person, use the techniques from this chapter to tell the truth. If presented in a positive way, honesty can strengthen your relationships and open the door to improved communication between you and others.

Tips: If you're not sure someone asking for "the truth" really wants it or is ready to handle it, ask. You might say, "Are you really sure you want me to give you feedback? I'm a pretty picky person." Or, "Are you sure you're ready to hear what I think? You seem pretty upset. Maybe we should discuss it tomorrow. When I'm upset, a little time allows me to gain better perspective, so I'm more open to what others think." Additionally, there will be times when people seek your input only to validate their own ideas. In those instances, after providing "the truth" the other party might say, "But what about X? Don't you think that's a better option?" Of course X is the thing he or she believed in the first place. If you get this response, you might say, "It sounds like you already know what you want to do. If you think that's best, then that's what you should do."

Chapter 19

Redirecting Poor Performance

G IVING feedback and being honest when things go well can be easy. Giving feedback when things don't go well can be more difficult. For one thing, many people are afraid of the reaction they'll get when they provide others with less-than-stellar feedback. Often, the reaction is defensiveness, anger, or even a reversal of the feedback that might include belittling the feedback or the person providing it. "Oh yeah? Well, I suppose you've never made a mistake." "What about you? You've been late to meetings before. In fact, you were ten minutes late last week!"

Although we can't control others' reactions to our feedback, phrasing the feedback in a way that is specific and focused on performance and results improves the odds that the feedback will be accepted in the spirit it was intended.

Performance Improvement Feedback has been called many things over the years—criticism, constructive criticism, feedback (while praise is considered a positive, feedback often has more negative connotations), coaching (which includes both positive and negative feedback and other communication), and more. The term "Performance Improvement Feedback" is used here for several reasons.

1. *It can help us decide when we should give feedback and when we should keep our thoughts to ourselves.*

If the feedback is not about the person's *performance* or given with the *intent* and *information* to help the person *change* that performance, then we probably should not be sharing it. That is the biggest difference between Performance Improvement Feedback and criticism. Criticism is negative feedback that doesn't give the recipient information about what he or she should do to fix the problem.

For example, should we tell a coworker we don't like his tie or her hairstyle? If neither person asked our opinion and if it is unrelated to improving job performance, it is simply criticism and most likely not appropriate.

2. It helps establish a mindset for the person providing the feedback.

Many people dread giving negative feedback or criticism because it makes everyone involved feel bad. The criticizer feels guilty and embarrassed and is sure the recipient will feel the same way. If we think about giving someone Performance Improvement Feedback, we can take away the negative connotation for both the recipient and ourselves. For instance, understanding beforehand that the feedback is intended to provide information that will make someone's job less stressful or improve productivity can help ensure it's provided properly and with the best intentions.

Going into a conversation with the mindset that we're providing people with information that will help them can change our whole approach. Additionally, the positive mindset affects our nonverbal communication. Instead of providing feedback while sheepishly looking at our shoes and verbally stumbling all over ourselves, we can look the person in the eye and deliver the helpful message.

When the goal is genuinely to help someone, the person receiving the feedback will likely notice those nonverbal cues and realize the true intent of the feedback. However, if the intent is simply to criticize, no matter how nicely stated, it's easy to notice those cues as well.

Effective Performance Improvement Feedback should contain three elements:

1. A specific description of the performance that needs improvement
2. A specific description of the results of the performance
3. Inquiring or advising how different actions could have provided a more positive outcome

1. A specific description of the performance that needs improvement

This means sharing the verbal and nonverbal behavior—specific things the person said and did that need to be changed or improved.

2. A specific description of the results of the performance

This means sharing consequences of the person's behavior. Understanding the negative consequences of the person's actions can be a strong motivator for change.

3. Inquiring or advising how different actions could have provided a more positive outcome

In some instances, it's best to ask people what they think they should do if faced with the same situation in the future. Asking allows the feedback receiver to be proactive and think about new behaviors in order to solve problems down the road. It can be a great learning opportunity. Other times, when someone is new or inexperienced and would be unable to think of alternative actions, it's best to simply come right out and explain what should be said and done in the future.

Performance Improvement Feedback: Inquiring

Devin: "Zack, I noticed when that customer was at the counter, you didn't make eye contact or let her know that you knew she was there. She seemed upset and said, 'Isn't anyone going to help me? I've been standing here five minutes.' I know you were busy entering the supply order, and I appreciate that you wanted to get it done. What could you have done differently to help avoid the complaint?"

Zack: "I guess I should have stopped entering the order and helped her right away or at least I should have told her I'd be with her in a minute."

Devin: "I think you're right. If you had acknowledged her, I think she might have been more patient. If you had stopped entering the order and helped her right away, she would have been even happier. I think that's a good plan for the next time that type of situation arises."

Performance Improvement Feedback: Advising

Devin: "Zack, I noticed when that customer came up to your counter, you didn't make eye contact or let her know that you knew she was there. It wasn't until she got upset and said, 'Isn't anyone going to help me? I've been standing here five minutes,' that you acknowledged her. I know you were busy entering the supply order in the computer, and I appreciate you trying to get that done early. However, we always want the needs of the customer to come first.

Next time, I'd like you to stop entering orders when a customer comes up to the counter. If you're not at a stopping point or are almost finished, you can just say, 'I'll be with you in a second,' and then get to a stopping point as quickly as you can. Either way, customers are less likely to get upset because they know you're going to help them shortly."

Another point to keep in mind: if we're going to provide feedback to a peer or someone else over whom we have no authority, it can be helpful to ask permission before proceeding in sharing the feedback.

> **Mike to Zack:** "That lady was really impatient. I know it's difficult to juggle customers and order entry. I've been doing this for a long time. Would you be interested in some tips that have helped me get orders entered and keep customers happy too?"

However, when we ask first, we're at risk for getting "no" as a response.

> **Mike:** "That lady was really impatient. I know it's difficult to juggle customers and order entry. I've been doing this for a long time. Would you be interested in some tips that have helped me get orders entered and keep customers happy too?"

> **Zack:** "No thanks. People will just have to wait until I'm done. They'll get over it."

Therefore, if we observe a person whose performance is unacceptable, and we need to address it, it may be best to avoid asking if they're interested in our input and simply go ahead and provide the feedback.

ACT on this chapter

Analyze: Take a look at your fears about giving Performance Improvement Feedback and face them. People cannot improve the things they can't see or don't know about. They need the help of those around them. Think about this type of feedback not as criticizing, but as helping others improve their characters.

Communicate: Change your perceptions about criticism and focus on what Performance Improvement Feedback means. Although it can be difficult to deliver at first, when we provide those around us with feedback that helps them work more efficiently, avoid conflict with customers, and otherwise reduce their stress, they may see the feedback as the gift we intend it to be.

Tips: If you wait too long to provide feedback, not only does the poor performance continue, but poor habits get harder to break because they become the norm for the other person. Feedback should be provided immediately whenever possible. If others are around, wait until you can share the information privately. If you are angry or upset and you can't approach the feedback positively, you should wait. However, try not to wait more than twenty-four hours because cool can quickly turn into cold feet, and you'll never deliver the feedback. Because the behavior goes unaddressed, it will likely happen again, and when it does, you'll likely approach the person with the "baggage" of the old feed-back that you never provided. That is unfair and often causes the feedback deliverer to be more emotional or upset than is warranted by the current situation.

Chapter 20

Delivering "Bad" News:
I Hate to Tell You This, But ...

PROVIDING feedback on job performance can be difficult. Providing personal feedback—feedback about body odor, bad breath, too much cologne, visible tattoos, piercings, or wrinkled, dirty, or inappropriate clothing—can be even more difficult.

When organizations have specific dress and appearance standards, addressing personal issues is somewhat easier. However, in many instances, dress and appearance standards are broad and vague. What exactly does "business casual," or "professional attire," really mean? Unless specifically defined, there can be many interpretations. When dress and appearance standards are nonexistent or vague, providing feedback on these issues can be very difficult.

In most instances, managers or the employee's supervisor should provide feedback on personal issues. However, the reality is that managers are often as uncomfortable addressing personal issues as anyone else, and in some instances, they don't work closely enough with the employee to know there's a problem. Therefore, the responsibility for having these conversations sometimes falls to coworkers, and in fact, there are some advantages to having a coworker address these issues rather than a manager, including:

- A coworker might be more able to approach the issue as a friend helping a friend.

- When a coworker addresses the issue directly, without elevating it to management, the feedback can seem less threatening and "official to the recipient."

- When a coworker addresses elevating it to management, the feedback can seem less threatening and "official" to the recipient.

- It avoids putting managers in the position of saying, "A little bird told me," or "I heard," when the feedback was reported to him or her.

The first step in giving personal feedback is to prepare ourselves for the likelihood of a defensive or negative response. Although this can happen with any "negative" feedback, it's more likely to occur with very personal feedback, because we're addressing a person's choices or habits. It's a lot easier for someone to hear, "The report you turned in is incomplete. It needs more statistics to back up your suggestions." In this kind of feedback, the report is taking the hit, the statistics are taking a hit, and the person is secondary. When you have to tell someone, "Your breath smells bad" or "Your perfume is making me sick," it's much harder for him or her to view the feedback objectively.

First, let's look at the things to avoid when addressing personal issues.

When providing personal feedback, we should:

1. Avoid sending e-mails or leaving anonymous "tips" on the person's desk.
2. Avoid the passive or passive-aggressive approach of dropping hints.
3. Avoid lying.
4. Avoid speaking for a group of coworkers.

1. Avoid sending e-mails or leaving anonymous "tips" on the person's desk.

Although an unsigned note or a bottle of mouthwash left on someone's desk might send the intended message, the person will likely be hurt and embarrassed, and won't know whom to trust. This embarrassment may cause him or her to withdraw from others or respond with angry accusations.

2. Avoid the passive or passive-aggressive approach of dropping hints.

Saying, "Wow, somebody has been eating garlic again" or "Whew, someone in here stole my Aunt Pearl's old lady perfume," will only cause the person to become embarrassed or defensive. That is, *if* the person realizes the comment is directed toward him or her. If the person doesn't get the hint, we're wasting our great-smelling breath.

3. Avoid lying.

If a customer *really* complained about a person's piercings or we *do* have allergies to cologne, then we should definitely let the person know. If not, then it's better to keep it to yourself. However, when being honest, we must still try to be as kind and considerate of the other person as we possibly can. For example, we don't have to tell our coworker that we think her perfume stinks, and we can't stand working next to her. We could just say that we're "sensitive" to certain colognes and perfumes and ask if she could please wear less or none at all. Using a vague term like "sensitive" is a good way to soften the blow of personal feedback but still avoid lying.

4. Avoid speaking for a group of coworkers.

Unless your coworkers have elected you as spokesperson for the group, you should only speak for yourself. Even if you were selected to represent the group, you should think about how the person receiving the feedback will feel when finding out that coworkers got together and discussed the problem behind his back. Unless you need "reinforcement" of the feedback, such as if the person says, "Well, that's just your opinion. No one else seems to have a problem with my cologne," you should just express your own viewpoint.

General guidelines for providing personal feedback:

1. Consider that personal issues such as body odor, cologne, facial hair, or piercings may be because of medical conditions, cultural reasons, or religious reasons.
2. Always provide personal feedback in private.
3. Discuss it only with the person who has the problem.
4. Avoid "always" and "never." Instead, use words such as "sometimes" or "lately."
5. Be honest about how you feel about delivering the feedback.
6. If you've had a similar problem in the past, share it.
7. Tell the person why he needs to know about the issue.
8. Let the person know that if the situation were reversed, you'd want to know if you had a problem.

1. Consider that personal issues such as body odor, cologne, facial hair, or piercings may be because of medical conditions, cultural reasons, or religious reasons.

If this is a possibility, we should consult with our organization's human resources department or legal office before addressing personal issues. It's not to say that we won't address the problem if it negatively affects customer service or productivity. However, we need to address it in a way that doesn't break any organizational policies or employment laws.

2. Always provide personal feedback in private.

Just like any negative feedback, very personal feedback should always be delivered in private. Not only is it more considerate, but people are much more receptive to very personal or embarrassing feedback if it is delivered privately.

3. Discuss it only with the person who has the problem.

Though it shouldn't have to be stated, personal issues should only be discussed with the person who has the problem. Sharing information with others is gossiping and does nothing to resolve the problem.

4. Avoid "always" and "never." Instead, use words such as "sometimes" or "lately."

If the person's tattoos have "always" scared customers, the person should have been told before now. The same goes for "never" ironing his or her clothes; something should have been said sooner.

5. Be honest about how you feel about delivering the feedback.

Admit that it's just as difficult or awkward to give this type of feedback as it likely is for the other person to hear.

6. If you've had a similar problem in the past, share it.

Sometimes it helps to admit if we've had a similar problem ourselves. For example, maybe at one time someone told us our perfume or cologne bothered someone else.

7. Tell the person why he needs to know about the issue.

It's important that people know we're only providing the feedback to help them be successful, not to nitpick or imply we're perfect.

8. Let the person know that if the situation were reversed, you'd want to know if you had a problem.

There are many things about ourselves to which we may be blind. Perhaps someday our own breath won't be as fresh as it could be, or our cologne will offend others. By letting someone know we would want to know about such problems, we let them know we are open to personal feedback, even if it is uncomfortable to give and receive.

"Doug, can we talk in the conference room for a minute? (Then, in the conference room) I need to share something that's been bothering me. I know I haven't mentioned it before, but I'm very sensitive to certain colognes. I don't know if I'm now just becoming sensitive to yours or if you recently changed it, but it's triggering my allergies. It would really help me if you didn't wear cologne to work, or at least not on days when we're working in the lab together."

"Dana, I've noticed when customers are checking out, they wait in line at other registers even if you don't have any customers. In fact, I approached someone today and told him that you were available to help, but he opted to stay in line. I think your lip and eyebrow rings may intimidate some of our more conservative customers, and I would appreciate it if you took them out when you're at work. It would help with traffic flow at the registers if more of our customers felt comfortable approaching you."

"Sue, I need to tell you something that's awkward for me to bring up and may be difficult for you to hear, but I know I would want you to tell me if the situation were reversed. Lately, your breath is not as fresh as it could be. We all have a problem with this sometimes, so I hope you'll let me know if my breath ever needs a little freshening."

"Greg, I know that presenting a professional image is important to you, so that's why I have to tell you something. This past week, your shirts and pants have been quite wrinkled. I know weather has been especially humid, but it's important that we look as neat and professional as possible. I've learned a few tricks since moving here that have helped me minimize wrinkles in this humid climate. If you're interested, I can let you in on my secrets."

There is, of course, a difference in the tone of the conversation when coming from an equal rather than a supervisor. While a supervisor can tell an employee that he or she must remove a nose ring or cease wearing strong perfume or cologne, personal feedback coming from a coworker allows room for requests or suggestions.

Even when using these gentle example phrases we might get a defensive response. People often react badly when they're embarrassed or caught off guard by feedback. If defensiveness occurs, we should just remain calm and reiterate relevant key points below:

- We're only sharing the information because we want the person to be successful.
- We'd want to know if we were in her shoes.
- We don't want to hurt her feelings.
- We're telling him because we consider him a friend.
- We're telling him because we don't want it to become a larger issue that customers might take to management.

Although not easy to do, providing personal feedback is often a necessary part of working with others. Even if the person is upset by the feedback, she'll probably be grateful in the end that you were brave enough, kind enough, or cared enough to let her know.

ACT on this chapter

Analyze: Thinking about the impact of personal habits gives us a great opportunity to analyze our own. Take a look in the mirror, give yourself the sniff-test, and think about your "bad habits" at work and at home. Doing a self-analysis might not only help you avoid being on the receiving end of personal feedback, but might help you become a coworker, family member, or friend, that people want to be around.

Communicate: Most likely, you won't find yourself having to provide very personal feedback often. However, look for opportunities to help those around you be more successful by providing personal feedback using the techniques in this chapter when it's truly necessary.

Tips: If you have let a known issue continue for a while without feedback, you cannot honestly say, "Lately, your clothes have been wrinkled," because the person will know it if he's never owned an iron and his clothes have always looked this way. To avoid lying, say, "I'm sorry I didn't tell you sooner," or, "This is partly my fault because I didn't tell you sooner." It allows you to be honest and has the additional benefit of softening the blow for the other person, since you're admitting your own imperfection or role in the problem persisting.

Chapter *21*

You Can Dish It,
But Can You Take It?

MANY people say they're open to feedback, but when they receive it, they don't respond in a way that reflects openness. As was stated in previous chapters, a common response to feedback is anger and defensiveness.

"Oh, I suppose you're perfect and you never make mistakes?"

"Me? What about David? He comes in late every day, and you never say anything to him."

"Oh yeah? Well, it only happened because you didn't provide me the statistics in time, which put me behind schedule!"

So what is it about feedback that's hard for so many of us to accept? In some instances, it's the embarrassment of "getting caught" doing something wrong, or having others notice and point out shortcomings. Other times, it's the way the feedback is delivered, whether face-to-face or via e-mail, in private or in public, or maybe the words used during delivery, or the nonverbal cues.

The first step in responding appropriately to feedback is to change how we look at it. Instead of perceiving it as criticism, finger pointing, or as an embarrassment, feedback should be seen as an opportunity to learn, at minimum, the provider's perception of us. It's also an opportunity to improve work, working relationships, and ourselves. So don't dread feedback, rather look at it as an opportunity to make a change for the better. Additionally, because it is difficult to get up the courage to tell someone when there's a problem, we should appreciate that she cares enough about us to overcome her fears and bring problems to our attention.

There are five steps for responding effectively to feedback:

1. Listen carefully without interrupting.
2. Paraphrase and ask clarifying questions.
3. If necessary, ask for time to think about the feedback.
4. Decide whether the feedback is valid.
5. Respond to the feedback provider, if necessary.

---

1. Listen carefully without interrupting.

It's difficult to respond to feedback if we haven't really listened. Admittedly, it's difficult to listen without interrupting if people criticize us in public, with sarcasm, or raise their voice. However, unless the situation is extremely hostile—in which case it's okay to tell people we're not willing to listen until they can provide the feedback calmly and without attacking—let feedback providers have their say and listen carefully to both their words and nonverbal messages.

> **Roger:** "Gary, you're just not a team player, you ..." (interrupted)
>
> **Gary:** "What do you mean I'm not a team player? I'm in here early every day, and I'm the last one to leave every night! I do more than my fair share!"

In this example, Gary should have let Roger continue his comments, and perhaps Roger would have elaborated on what he meant by, "not a team player." When people provide feedback, they may often use broad terms that need to be clarified, such as:

"You're not being a team player."

"You're not doing your fair share."

"I can't count on you."

"You were rude to that customer."

Ideally, Roger should have avoided the label "team player" and provided Gary with a specific description of the behavior he felt was causing a problem. It's possible he would have gotten to specifics if Gary had heard him out. If not, Gary could paraphrase or ask questions to clarify what Roger meant by "you're not a team player."

2. Paraphrase and ask clarifying questions.

Restating the feedback and the emotion that was expressed either verbally or nonverbally lets the feedback provider know what we understood and gives him or her a chance to clarify the feedback. Additionally, asking clarifying questions can help us obtain more information that the provider may not have thought to include:

"Roger, I'm sorry you feel I'm not being a team player. Can you tell me what you mean by that? What specifically have I said or done that makes you feel I'm not a team player?"

Other clarifying questions include:

"Can you give me a specific example?"

"Is it because of (provide your own example)?"

"How did my behavior affect you?"

"What would you have done in my place?"

3. If necessary, ask for time to think about the feedback.

In some instances, the first two steps above will provide us with enough information to make a decision about the feedback. In other instances, we may need more time to think about the feedback before accepting, rejecting, or responding to it. Emotions can cloud judgment and stand in the way of an appropriate response, or there may be a need to go back and check facts or information before making a decision about the feedback. Either way, it's okay to ask for time to think about the feedback.

> "I'm glad you let me know how you feel. I need some time to think about what you've said. Can we talk about this again tomorrow morning?"

> "I'm glad you brought this to my attention. I'll need to go back to my office to check my statistics before I can respond. Can you give me an hour and I'll call you back?"

If we take time to think about the feedback, it's important that we respond within an "acceptable" amount of time. Waiting days or weeks to get back with someone will leave them feeling that we're ignoring the feedback or are indifferent.

4. Decide whether the feedback is valid.

Sometimes assessing the validity of feedback is based on fact. For example, if someone says there are typos in a report and points out several examples, there's not much else to do but:

- Admit the mistake and correct it.
- Thank the person for bringing the mistake to our attention.
- Determine, and possibly share with the feedback provider how the mistake will be avoided in the future.
- Move on.

Sometimes feedback is not "black and white" and is harder to assess. For example, a coworker might say he notices that we talk too loudly to customers on the phone and that our customers might feel like we're yelling at them. Or someone might tell us we should go about our work in a different way than we normally do. In these instances, we have to ask a few questions to decide whether to accept or reject the feedback. If we accept the feedback, we would change aspects of our behavior. If we reject the feedback, we would continue doing what we've always done.

In deciding whether to accept or reject feedback, it's helpful to ask ourselves a few questions to put the feedback in perspective.

Is the feedback something we've heard from others?

If this is the first and only time anyone has provided feedback about being too loud, then it could be considered an isolated incident or just one person's opinion, in which case, rejecting it might be a valid conclusion. If it's an issue that has been raised before and we ignored it, now might be the time to be honest and realize there's a problem. Additionally, even if it is the first time to receive this feedback, it's never a bad idea to ask someone else if it's valid. By approaching another coworker and saying, "Someone mentioned that they thought I might talk too loudly to customers and may seem to be yelling. You've heard me on the phone. What do you think? I certainly don't want my customers to think I'm rude or aggressive." It may turn out that the feedback is valid, but no one wanted to be the one to tell the truth before now.

Does the feedback provider have the knowledge and experience necessary to provide valid feedback?

We wouldn't take driving instructions from a toddler riding in the back seat or ask someone who doesn't speak or write Spanish to evaluate the Spanish version of an instruction manual. When evaluating feedback, we must consider whether the person giving it has the experience, education, or other qualifications to evaluate our behavior fairly. If the feedback giver is unqualified, it may be unwise to accept the feedback. If he or she is qualified, we should consider accepting the feedback. However, just because someone is an expert doesn't necessarily mean the feedback is valid. If after asking this question we're still undecided, we can use the answers to the other questions to make a decision about accepting or rejecting the feedback.

Is the feedback appropriately timed?

Many people won't take the time to provide feedback before a task has been done, but have no problem playing "Monday Morning Quarterback" after the fact. When feedback comes after the fact and we cannot act on that feedback, rejecting the feedback may be acceptable.

For example, last Monday, Sue asked Tony to provide input on the layout and design of a new company brochure. Tony said, "Whatever you pick is fine with me; I don't care."

This Monday, when the brochures arrived, Tony came to Sue's office and said, "I can't believe you picked orange for the brochure. Red would have been a much better color."

It would be acceptable for Sue to reject the feedback, saying, "Tony, I'm sorry you don't like the colors, but I gave you the chance to provide input before they were printed. I'm satisfied with the way they turned out."

Is the feedback factual or just a different opinion?

Taking the timing out of the scenario above, even if Tony had taken the time to review the brochure and disagreed with the color choice, that doesn't necessarily mean Sue should change her color choice. Just because someone has a different opinion doesn't mean we have to change our direction. In these instances, it's a judgment call whether to go with our own opinions, accept the other person's opinion, or ask for input from other people. If it's an issue we feel strongly about, we'll likely reject the feedback. If the issue isn't important to us but is important to the other person, we may "accept" the criticism and make a change. Feedback doesn't have to be seen as an order, but rather could be viewed as a recommendation or even merely an alternate point of view.

Is the feedback truly about this issue, or is the provider upset about something else?

People sometimes criticize because they're angry or upset about another situation and we just happen to be the first person they come across. In these instances, not only is it acceptable to reject the feedback, but also to let the person providing feedback know that we're sorry he or she is upset, but that

we don't appreciate being the target of frustration. Other times the feedback provider may be angry or upset with us about something unrelated or in the past. Asking specific questions and paraphrasing what we hear can often help identify the real problem.

Does the feedback provider have unrealistic expectations?

Sometimes people have impossibly high standards that are unrealistic given the circumstances. In other instances, the feedback provider may just be overly critical. For example, a coworker may want to miss a deadline in order to perfect a project when perfection is unattainable and unnecessary. In situations such as these, it's often best to reject the feedback. We shouldn't confuse a lack of perfectionism with laziness. Rather, we are being realistic, given our time, cost, or other constraints, about what can be done. If we can't do more, the feedback isn't practical.

5. Respond to the feedback provider, if necessary.

When feedback is simply a suggestion, there's no need to respond specifically as to whether you will or will not take the suggestion. It may be enough to verify that you've received the feedback by saying, "You've given me something to think about. I appreciate you letting me know what you think."

At other times, it's important to explain that we understand the feedback and what we plan to do in response to it.

> *"Jim, I went back and reviewed my notes and redid all the calculations. I found the errors and corrected them. In the future, I'll have you look at them before I send them to a customer. Thanks for letting me know about the mistakes."*

> *"David, I understand your concern about the number of brochures we printed, and if I had the budget, I would have printed more as you suggested. Unfortunately, I only have*

$450 in my printing budget, so I can only print 1,500 copies each quarter."

"Thanks for showing me how you prep your quarterly report Mary. It's another effective way to get it done, and I'm glad it works for you. However, because my method works just as quickly for me and gets good results, I think I'm going to stick with my old method. Thank you for showing me though. It's good to know there are other options."

Finally, there are times when people, either intentionally or without thinking, choose public settings to provide feedback. In these situations, it's best to let them know how and when we would prefer to receive feedback in the future.

"Harry, I'm glad you caught my error in the proposal before it was submitted to the client. Would you do me a favor though? The next time you find a mistake, give me a call, or e-mail me before the staff meeting. That way I can fix it and avoid the embarrassment of hearing about it in front of others at the meeting."

ACT on this chapter

Analyze: Most of us are blind to the many behaviors we exhibit that could be improved. If we were aware of these behaviors, we would have fixed them by now, right? Although not always easy to hear, we should all change the way we view being on the receiving end of feedback and should see it as the opportunity that it is.

Communicate: Show your openness to feedback by responding to it using the guidelines from this chapter. Remember, even though just one person may have been brave enough to say it, ten others might be thinking the same thing. Although feedback can sometimes be difficult to receive, wouldn't you rather know what people are thinking about you rather than them keeping it to themselves or sharing it with others—maybe your boss? Finally, when you receive feedback, even if not expertly or properly delivered, be sure to accept it graciously. Then let the other party know how you'd like to receive feed-back in the future.

Tips: If you find yourself having a hard time accepting feed-back because you don't know how to respond or aren't sure if the feedback is accurate, ask questions to get more information or ask for some time to think about the feedback before responding. Ensuring that you have all the information you need and taking some time to think about what you've heard, helps ensure that you respond to the feedback logically and appropriately.

Chapter 22

Answering the Telephone Professionally

THE way we answer the telephone is a reflection of our organization and ourselves. It's also the first impression we give first-time callers.

"City Hall, can I help you?"

"Doctor's office ..."

"Ha, ha, ha, that's so funny ..." (Obviously mid-conversation with a coworker when picking up the phone). "Oh, uh, hello, First Bank. This is Stacey. How can I help you today?"

The examples above range from incomplete to unprofessional. They don't help callers determine if they have reached the organization or department they are attempting to call. Professional telephone etiquette is simple if we just prepare for calls before answering the telephone and remember a few simple tips once we do.

To answer the telephone professionally:

1. Be prepared and focused before picking up the telephone.
2. Don't allow the phone to ring more than three times before answering.
3. Smile before picking up the telephone.
4. Use a prepared, standardized telephone opener.

1. Be prepared and focused before picking up the telephone.

If we are mid-conversation with a coworker, we need to end the conversation before picking up the phone. The same goes for eating. People who eat lunch at their desks should get a lot of credit for their dedication. However, callers shouldn't have to hear the noises and deal with the delay while someone tries to choke down a mouthful of sandwich before speaking. Be sure to finish chewing and talking with others, take a deep breath, and *then* answer the phone.

2. Don't allow the phone to ring more than three times before answering.

Letting a phone ring more than three times creates the impression that an organization is understaffed or otherwise unprepared to help. If we're ready to answer sooner, so much the better. However, sometimes it takes three rings to ready ourselves.

3. Smile before picking up the telephone.

This is an important detail despite the fact that the caller can't see our faces. A smile causes a person's vocal qualities to change. When we smile, the pitch of our voices raises and we sound more pleasant than we would if we weren't smiling.

Don't believe it? Try looking in the mirror and saying the following: "I like you very much." The first time, say it without smiling. Then, say it again while wearing a big smile. Hear the difference? The second time should sound much more pleasant than the first.

4. Use a prepared, standardized telephone opener.

All employees in an organization should use the same telephone opener when answering calls. Using a good telephone opener makes a great first impression on callers and lets them know exactly who they've reached in what organization and in what department.

A professional telephone opener includes the following:

1. A greeting: "Good morning" or "Good afternoon."
2. The employee's name, organization name, and department name
3. The question: "How may I help you?"

"Good morning, Northside Hospital radiology department. This is Terry Farrell. How may I help you?"

"Good afternoon, Noah's Ark Animal Clinic. This is Dan Reynolds. How may I help you?"

"Good morning, ABC Educational Supplies, order department. This is Ann Craven. How may I help you today?"

Short, sweet, and professional—these openers let callers know exactly what organization and department they've reached, to whom they are speaking, and that the person who answered is ready to help. It's always best to say "How may I help you?" rather than "Can I help you?" The former says we're ready and waiting to help callers as soon as they tell us what they need. The latter implies that we're unsure and relying on our callers to tell us whether we can help.

Finally, excellent telephone etiquette is just as important as good communication in face-to-face situations, maybe more so because it provides callers with their first impression of us and our organization.

ACT on this chapter

Analyze: Think about how you and others around you answer the telephone. Are you taking every opportunity to make a great first impression on your callers? Or does the way you answer the phone cause confusion? If callers have to ask, "Is this XYZ, Inc.?" or, "May I ask your name please?" then your telephone opener might need to be revised.

Communicate: Using the guidelines from this chapter for answering the telephone efficiently and professionally will create a great first impression for those who call your organization. Even when things get busy, take time to focus before answering the phone. A first call could be the last if callers get a poor impression.

Tips: Keep your telephone opener posted near your phone so you'll always be consistent in answering calls. Be sure, especially if you are a supervisor, to pay attention to how others in your organization answer the phone too. All your hard work creating a good impression could be undone by an employee or coworker who answers the phone poorly. If you are a supervisor, provide your employees with a script for an opener you want them to use. Perhaps practice the openers during a staff meeting, so everyone can hear how others sound when they answer the phone. Make note of those whose voices project the cheerful and professional image you want for your organization.

Creating an Effective Voicemail Greeting

HOW we answer the phone can make a positive or negative first impression on those who call us. The voicemail greeting we record for callers to hear when we don't answer the phone can provide the same experience. What type of impression does the following greetings leave?

> *"This is Bob Smith, I'm out of the office doing some important stuff and don't have time to talk to you right now. I'll call you back when I feel like it." (beep)*

> *"Hi! It's Suzy! I'm not available to take your call. I'm either in a meeting, or out of the office, at a doctor's appointment, running an errand, or I might be on vacation. Leave your info and I'll get back to you at my earliest convenience." (beep)*

> *"Hey! It's Ned. Surprise, surprise! You've reached my voicemail. You know what to do." (beep)*

Probably not the professional impression these employees' bosses want left with their callers. What's wrong with these greetings?

Bob's greeting is condescending and leaves callers, possibly his customers, with the impression that they are his last priority. In addition, it doesn't let callers know where he is, when he'll be back, or when they'll hear back from him.

Suzy's greeting wastes time telling callers she's not able to take their calls, then rambles on about all the possible places she could be. It ends with a nice way of saying, "I'll call you back when I feel like it." There's no need in her voicemail greeting to state the obvious— that she's not in. Because the caller reached her voicemail, the caller probably figured as much!

The often-used and incorrect phrase, "I'll return calls at my earliest convenience," is also a waste of time. What does that mean? In a week, a month, or next year? It also leaves callers with the impression that Suzy prioritizes herself and her convenience over the people who call her, which is not the impression she probably wants to leave with customers who call.

Ned's greeting doesn't tell callers much of anything. Besides, telling callers, "You know what to do" is an invitation for them to leave anything and everything in a message, not necessarily the information he needs to help them.

A voicemail greeting should be planned, rehearsed, and should provide callers with necessary information. Additionally, voicemail greetings must be updated to reflect the status of the message recipient. This may require us to update our greeting on a daily basis or, at a minimum, when we're going to be out of the office for several hours or several days.

When we will be unavailable for an extended period, taking the time to update our greetings actually saves us time wading through dozens of messages later on. When callers know we're out of the office for the day, or a week, they won't call us repeatedly during that time. They'll either leave a message and wait for us to call back at the time stated in our greeting, or they'll contact the person we've designated to help them in the interim.

An effective voicemail greeting should include the following:

1. The recipient's name, department or position, and organization
2. Date of recording
3. Date and time the recipient will be back in the office or return calls
4. Whether the recipient will check messages during the absence (as necessary)
5. Options for contacting someone else who can help in the interim
6. Exactly what information should be left by the caller

"This is Anne Castillo, human resources director for Appletree Education. It's June 3rd and I am attending a workshop today. I will be back in my office tomorrow at 8:00 AM and will return calls before noon. If you need help in the interim, please call Janice Timmons at 800-555-0987. Otherwise, please leave your name, purpose of your call, best time to call you back, and the best number to call to reach you. Thank you!"

Anne's greeting tells callers exactly whose voicemail they've reached and lets them know they won't hear from her until tomorrow at earliest. It also provides an alternate contact if they can't wait until tomorrow. Finally, it tells callers exactly what information they should leave so she can help them when she returns their calls.

To make the most of her voicemail greeting, Anne did the following:

1. She wrote out her greeting to make certain she used the minimum number of words in her greeting. No one wants to listen to a long voicemail greeting. Writing the greeting out in advance helps ensure we get all the key information in the greeting in as short a message as possible.

2. She practiced reading her greeting aloud to ensure she spoke clearly in the recording, and that she didn't stumble over her words. Practicing also ensured she was able to include all the information above in a relatively short timeframe.

3. She smiled before she began reading her greeting, so her voice would sound pleasant and professional.

4. When recording, she enunciated her words to be sure she was easily understood.

5. Finally, once she recorded the greeting, she listened to it a few times to ensure it was clear, professional, and included all necessary information.

ACT on this chapter

Analyze: Call your phone number to listen to the voicemail greeting others hear when they call you. Do you sound enthusiastic and professional or like a bored robot? Does your greeting include all necessary information? Is it updated or does it still say you're out of office attending last year's annual trade show?

Communicate: Make the most of your voicemail greeting so it communicates necessary information and helps you make a positive impression on everyone who calls you. If necessary, record a new voicemail greeting today using the guidelines from this chapter. Remember to update your voicemail, whenever you'll be out of the office, but especially when you'll be gone for an extended period.

Tips: Write down or set up an electronic reminder to update your voicemail greeting each time you add an appointment or vacation to your calendar. Also, set up a reminder to change the message upon your return. If you write out your greeting before recording it, you can ensure it includes all relevant information and is as short and direct as possible. Practice reading the greeting aloud before recording it to avoid stumbling over your words when recording the message. Finally, remember to smile and speak clearly, so your message sounds positive and professional, and be sure to slow down when providing alternate contacts' phone numbers, to give callers time to write the numbers down.

Chapter 24

Voicemail Messages That Get Results

MANY people can relate to the frustration of receiving a voicemail message that is unclear, incomplete, or so longwinded that they don't even listen to the whole thing. Alternatively, we can also relate to the frustration of leaving a message for someone only to have them call back and ask, "What did you want?" because the recipient didn't listen to the message.

Leaving an effective voicemail message that people will listen and respond to is not an art; it's a simple process of following a few guidelines for effective messaging. First, it's important to be prepared to leave a message in the event we don't reach the person we're calling.

> *"Oh, um, hi Brenda. It's Devin. I, uh, was calling because I had a few questions about the e-mail you sent me with the proposal that's due … (Beep! Message ended.)*

If we're not prepared to leave a short, clear message, the voicemail system will likely cut us off before we get to the point. Second, although we want to leave brief messages, we don't want to be so brief that the person we're calling doesn't know who we are, what we want, or how to get in contact with us.

Mystery Caller: "Hi Carrie, it's me. Give me a call. I have a few questions for you. Thanks."

Even if Carrie recognizes the voice as Dave's and has his telephone number, this too-brief message will likely cause her to make two return phone calls. The first to find out what he needs, and the second to call with the needed information. Because Carrie didn't know what he needed in the first place, it's unlikely she'll have it at hand when she calls him back.

> **Carrie:** "Dave, its Carrie from ABC Shipping. I got your message. What questions did you have?"
>
> **Dave:** "Thanks for calling me back Carrie. I need to know when you shipped two of our orders. I have the order numbers if you need them."
>
> **Carrie:** "Sure Dave, give me the order numbers then I'll have to go check the shipping records and call you back with the ship date."

If Dave had provided the order numbers and asked when the orders shipped in his first message, Carrie would have been able to call him back with the information on the first return call.

It shouldn't be a surprise when we call people and reach their voicemail. Most people don't spend their entire day at their desks. We should be prepared to leave a voicemail message and should be pleasantly surprised if we actually do get the recipient "live." Even if the person we call does answer the phone, being prepared with a message will help to ensure that we get to the point quickly, making the call as efficient as possible. This doesn't mean we have to write a script of the call, but we should at least have an idea of the key issues or questions we want to discuss.

A good voicemail message should include the following:

1. The caller's name, organization name, and contact information
2. A brief, specific message, beginning with "I need ..."
3. Motivation to call back (if necessary)
4. Best time to return the call
5. The caller's name and number, at minimum, at the beginning and end of the message

"Hello. This is John Pope of ABC Incorporated. My telephone number is (pause) 800-555-1234. I need the installation specifications for two of your products: (pause) product #123, the Mighty Widget, and product #877, the Super Whatchamacallit. The best time to reach me today is between 1:00 and 3:00 PM. Again, this is John Pope at ABC. I can be reached at (pause) 800-555-1234."

This message tells the recipient exactly who called, where the caller works, how to get back in touch with him, and exactly what he needs. By pausing before stating his phone number, John gives the message recipient a chance to grab a pen and write down his number. Repeating his name and number at the end of the message gives the recipient a second chance to verify that he or she wrote down the name and number correctly.

Additionally, when leaving a telephone number, we should try to say the number as slowly as the time it would take to write it down. Many people leave their phone number only once and so quickly that no one could possibly copy it down without having to listen to the message multiple times. These same people often leave their numbers at the end of messages, forcing recipients to listen to the entire message multiple times to catch the number.

In the previous example, John is a customer of the organization he's called. There should be some intrinsic motivation for the recipient to call him back. In other instances, we may need to provide motivation for the recipient to call us back.

"Hello. This is John Pope of ABC Incorporated. My telephone number is 800-555-1234. The credit card number you used to place your order online was missing a number. Please call me before 3:00 PM with the complete number so we can ship your order today. Again, this is John Pope. My phone number is 800-555-1234."

This message provides John's customer with motivation to call him back by 3:00 PM. If the customer doesn't call by 3:00 PM, the order won't be shipped today. If John had simply left a message with his name and number and said, "Please call me back," the customer may not have called today, the order would be delayed, and the customer would probably be unhappy.

Another guideline for leaving an effective voicemail message is to try to keep the message to less than sixty seconds. We should only leave a longer message if in doing so, we avoid requiring the recipient to call us back twice.

Finally, are there times when we shouldn't leave a detailed or longer message? Yes. If the details are of a personal or private nature, we wouldn't want to leave a message for someone stating:

> "Mrs. Smith, we got your dog's test results. He's got six months to live."

> "Alan, I'm sorry to be the one to tell you this, but you're being laid off. Don't bother coming in tomorrow."
> "Mr. Jones, you didn't pay your bill this month, so we're cutting off your water at noon today."

> "Mr. Clark, your check bounced, so we'll need you to come in and pay cash."

In these instances, it would be best to leave a simple message stating that we need to speak to the recipient without stating the specific purpose of our call.

Another instance when we wouldn't want to leave a longer message is if we have so many questions that a message would go on for ten minutes. Remember, we're trying to keep messages to around sixty seconds. In an instance where we just can't cover it all in around sixty seconds, try the following:

> *"I have several questions about building my Web site. Please call me back when you have about fifteen minutes to talk."*

ACT on this chapter

Analyze: Think about all the long voicemail messages you've received in your life, as well as those that were so incomplete that you couldn't even return the call. Now think about the results of those messages. Not only were they frustrating to you, but they might have cost you or the caller a job, contract, or some other opportunity because the messages weren't thought out well.

Communicate: In the coming days, start the good habit of planning what you'll say if you get a live person or voice-mail before you pick up the phone. Jot down a few key points or questions you have as well as any necessary motivation for someone to call you back. Be sure the messages you leave include your name, organization, and phone number at the beginning and end of the message. Speak slowly, especially when giving your telephone number, and remember to enunciate. Finally, do not leave personal or private information in a message. Simply ask the recipient to call you as soon as possible.

Tips: When in doubt about whether your message will be too long, too vague, easily misinterpreted, or inappropriate, don't leave a message. Although some voicemail systems allow callers to review, erase, and re-record their message, not all do. Call back later and reach the person directly, so you can provide additional detail, ask questions, or respond to questions, than to leave an "inappropriate" message.

Chapter 25

E-mail Subject Lines
That Get Attention

ACCORDING to recent studies, billions of e-mails are sent every second, and employees send and receive nearly two hundred e-mail messages each day. As a result, people don't read many of the messages they receive, or at least don't read them in a timely manner. As a coping technique, recipients will scan an e-mail's subject line to decide whether to delete it, open and read it immediately, or read the message later. The most common mistakes people make regarding subject lines that can cause their e-mails to go unread include:

1. *Not including a subject line, one-word subject lines, or vague subject lines*

Telling recipients little or nothing about the content of an e-mail is not likely to compel them to open and read the message.

2. *A subject line that screams "URGENT!" when the content is less than urgent*

Act Now! Last Chance! Emergency! Once recipients realize this is our technique to get them to open e-mails, they'll no longer open them. Additionally, depending on the words we use to express our urgency, the recipient's spam filter may identify the e-mail as junk and move it to the spam folder.

3. Subject lines that contain spam keywords

Many spam filters will screen out e-mails with subject lines containing spam keywords, such as "free," "money," "deal," "survey," and "sign-up." Therefore, avoid using these terms in e-mail subject lines.

4. Generic subject lines that aren't personalized to the recipient

If the subject line reads like a mass mailing, rather than an e-mail customized to the recipient, it will likely be read last, if at all.

5. Asking for help or making requests

People want to know what's in it for them. People are busy and have their own priorities, which generally don't include seeking to take on other people's work. Therefore, if an e-mail subject line only reads, "Need your help," the e-mail is likely to be the last one opened, if it's opened at all. Additionally, people may ignore a help-seeking e-mail sent to multiple recipients because they assume someone else will help.

If we want people to read the e-mails we write, the first step is to write subject lines that motivate them to open our e-mails right away. Unfortunately, many people don't know how to write a subject line that gets people's attention.

To write an effective e-mail subject line, use the following guidelines:

1. Keep subject lines to no more than fifty-two characters, including spaces.
2. Summarize the bottom line of the e-mail's message.
3. If you have a question and it fits in the subject line, put it there.
4. If a recipient has something to gain by opening, or lose by not opening an e-mail, state so in the subject line.
5. Split e-mails with multiple topics into multiple e-mails, so that each subject line reflects the content of the e-mail.
6. If a message requires some action on the part of the recipient, state the action in the subject line.
7. Avoid unnecessary words, such as adjectives and adverbs.

1. Keep subject lines to no more than fifty-two characters, including spaces.

Most people can only see fifty-two to fifty-six characters of the subject line when previewing their e-mail list. The rest of the subject line is only visible when the recipient opens the e-mail. By keeping subject lines to fifty-two characters or fewer, we can safely assume recipients will be able to read most, if not all, of the subject line.

2. Summarize the bottom line of the e-mail's message.

A good subject line is like a good newspaper headline. It lets the reader know the overriding message of the body of the e-mail.

Example: *15 Employees chosen for Management Academy*

3. *If you have a question and it fits in the subject line, put it there.*

There's no need to have a subject line that reads, "Have a question for you," and then write, "What's your cell phone number?" in the body of the e-mail. Why not just put, "What's your cell phone number?" in the subject line and keep the body of the e-mail blank? This way, the recipient doesn't even have to open the e-mail to know what you want.

Example: *Can you call me at 832-111-1234 by 3:00 PM?*

4. *If a recipient has something to gain by opening, or lose by not opening an e-mail, state so in the subject line.*

If you can provide motivation to open the e-mail in your subject line, the odds are, people will open the e-mail and read it. Again, don't provide false urgency, but e-mail subject lines that include deadlines or motivation to open them get opened.

Example: *Benefit sign up deadline 2/7: Instructions inside*

5. *Split e-mails with multiple topics into multiple e-mails so each subject line reflects the content of the e-mail.*

No one wants to open an e-mail with a subject line that reads, "Lots of questions," or "Several issues of concern." Subject lines like these are not only unappealing, but make it difficult for recipients to find the correct e-mail later if they need to refer back to a specific "issue" that was included.

6. *If a message requires some action on the part of the recipient, state the action in the subject line.*

Especially when the action is time sensitive, it's important to state the action in the subject line, so the recipient immediately knows what the action is and when it must be completed.

Example: *Sign and return attached proposal by 11/22.*

7. Avoid unnecessary words, such as adjectives and adverbs.

We shouldn't use slang or incorrect abbreviations in e-mail subject lines, and it's also okay to **exclude** adjectives and adverbs. Do we really need to say something is "very good" or is "good" good enough? Cutting extraneous words will help keep the word count down in our subject lines.

Poor: *Proposal*

Better: *E-mail etiquette training proposal you requested*

———————

Poor: *Timecards*

Better: *Timecards due by 5:00 PM today*

———————

Poor: *Really Fantastic E-mail Etiquette Training Class*

Better: *E-mail etiquette class: Register by Oct. 1*

———————

Poor: *Question for you*

Better: *What time does the staff meeting start tomorrow?*

———————

Poor: *New Client*

Better: *XYZ, Inc., signed contract—work begins 11/01*

———————

Poor: *Forms*

Better: *Please sign attached forms and return by 12/7*

───────────

Poor: *Our Meeting*

Better: *Summary of agreements from 6/1 meeting*

ACT on this chapter

Analyze: Take time to review the e-mail messages you sent and received over the last week. Did you or the other senders make the most of your subject lines? If not, take note of how they could be improved, so you can make appropriate changes in the future.

Communicate: Before sending e-mails this week, be sure to review your subject lines to ensure they meet the criteria in this chapter. Additionally, take the opportunity to help your coworkers by suggesting improvements when they send e-mails with subject lines that are vague or misleading. To soften the feedback, you might suggest that with the volume of e-mails you receive, it would be helpful if the sender could be more specific in the subject lines to ensure you read his or her e-mails.

Tips: Because this chapter consists of tips for effective subject lines, it's a great idea to use those tips and guidelines to create a checklist that you can post by your computer, so you can review it before you press "send" on that next e-mail. Consider e-mails you typically discard without reading because of vague or overly complicated subject lines. Avoid those pitfalls in your own e-mails.

Conclusion

I wasn't born a great communicator. Growing up, an "argument" consisted of a test of who could come up with the worst, most ugly thing to say, so that the other person was so dumbfounded he or she couldn't respond. Yea, I win!

25 years later, after two communication degrees, writing books and blogs on the subject, and speaking to thousands of people about communication, I am a much better communicator. However, I still need to work at it every day. Even if you KNOW how to do something, you still need to CHOOSE to do it.

I began my communication journey with a limited set of tools. I often describe it as the "fisher price" starter set. You know, the one with three little plastic tools- a hammer, screwdriver, and wrench. After 25 years, my toolbox has grown. I have added more durable, sophisticated, and fine-tuned tools and I plan to continue to add any tools that will help me "get along and get it done."

Great communication skills are learned. We're not born with them. We must seek them out, be open to them when we receive them, and practice them until they become second nature. It takes time and work, but it's worth it. With each new tool you acquire, you take a step toward clearer communication, better working and personal relationships, improved productivity, and success.

Focus on one skill and practice it until you master it. Then set your next goal and keep growing. Improving communication skills is hard work, but I promise, it will be one of the most rewarding things you do for yourself in your life.

   –   Amy Castro

About the Author

Amy P. Castro is a recognized performance communication expert, author, blogger, and President of Innovative Communication & Training Solutions, and proud U.S. Air Force Veteran. She has more than twenty years of experience in communication and training for business, the federal government, and higher education. She is recognized for her abilities in all areas of workplace communication including oral and written communication, customer service, coaching, conflict resolution, presentation and facilitation skills, and leadership/management skills.

Amy holds a Bachelor's Degree in Journalism from the George Washington University and a Master's Degree in Communication Studies from the University of Northern Colorado.

As a speaker, Amy uses her down-to-earth style, REAL stories, humor, and fun to create customized and engaging workshops, keynotes, and breakout sessions, focused on **Performance Communication** which she defines as, **"Assertive communication that is Positive, Purposeful, and Practical."** Her goal is for participants to leave her programs ready to easily put new communication skills into action.

Before founding ICTS, Amy served for four years in the U.S. Air Force and was the deputy chief of public affairs and the chief of media relations at Peterson Air Force Base in Colorado Springs, Colorado. As an Air Force Captain, she performed communication and media-relations activities and was responsible for advising and training senior Air Force officers as well as mid-level and junior staff members in media interviewing, presentation skills and persuasion.

Amy holds a master's degree in human communication from the University of Northern Colorado and a bachelor's degree in journalism from The George Washington University.

Contact Amy through her website at www.Amy-Castro.com, or via email at Amy@Amy-Castro.com.

Made in the USA
Monee, IL
17 April 2021